MEMORIES FROM THE HEART OF HOCKEYTOWN

THE JOE

WELCOME TO JOE LOUIS ARENA   HOME OF THE DETROIT RED WINGS

Joe Louis Arena

THE LINEUP

EDITOR
Gene Myers
DESIGNER
Ryan Ford
COPY EDITORS
Jennifer Troyer
Marlowe Alter
Tim Marcinkoski
PHOTO EDITING
Ryan Ford
PHOTO IMAGING
Jeff Tarsha
FREE PRESS SPORTS DIRECTOR
Kevin Bull
SPECIAL THANKS
Noah Amstadter
Kris Anstrats
Viv Bernstein
Patrick Byrne
Steve Byrne
Bernie Czarniecki
Owen Davis
Keith Gave
Megan Holt
Robert Huschka
Brian McCollum
Beth Myers
Dora Robles Hernandez
Jacki Shipley
George Sipple
The Anchor Bar
IN MEMORIAM
Drew Sharp

On the cover

FRONT: PHOTO BY RICK OSENTOSKI/ USA TODAY SPORTS; BACK: PHOTO BY MARY SCHROEDER/DFP

‹‹ On Page 1

JOE LOUIS ARENA EXTERIOR PHOTO BY MARY SCHROEDER/DETROIT FREE PRESS

On Page 3 ››

1984 MIKE ILITCH AT JOE LOUIS ARENA PHOTO BY JOHN COLLIER/DETROIT FREE PRESS

The dawn of Hockeytown

Spring of 1984. Steve Yzerman and Lane Lambert. Promising rookies. Center and right wing. Potential linemates for years. Drafted fourth, Yzerman led the Red Wings with 87 points (39 goals, 48 assists). Drafted 25th, Lambert was eighth with 35 points (20 goals, 15 assists). The Wings, in their second year under owner Mike Ilitch and general manager Jimmy Devellano, made the playoffs. First time in six years. Second time in 17 years. Still finished 11 games under .500 with 69 points, but no longer the Dead Wings. Joe Louis Arena, 4½ years old, once half-empty, now mostly full. Winning of Stanley Cups and concept of Hockeytown unimaginable. But, at last, hope. The future: Hall of Fame for Yzerman, Ilitch and Devellano. Three Cups in six seasons, four in 11. Six Cup finals in 14 seasons. Playoff berths in 25 consecutive seasons. Lambert? Traded two years later. Only 283 career NHL games. But played in the minors past the turn of the century. Can't win 'em all.
MARY SCHROEDER/DETROIT FREE PRESS

TRIUMPH BOOKS

TRIUMPHBOOKS.COM
@TriumphBooks

This is an unofficial publication. This book is in no way affiliated with, licensed by, or endorsed by the Detroit Red Wings or the NHL.

Detroit Free Press

160 W. Fort St., Detroit, MI 48226
www.freep.com

A GANNETT COMPANY

This book is available in quantity at special discounts for your group or organization. For further information, contact: Triumph Books LLC, 814 North Franklin Street, Chicago, Illinois 60610 Phone: (312) 337-0747; Web: www.triumphbooks.com; Twitter: @TriumphBooks

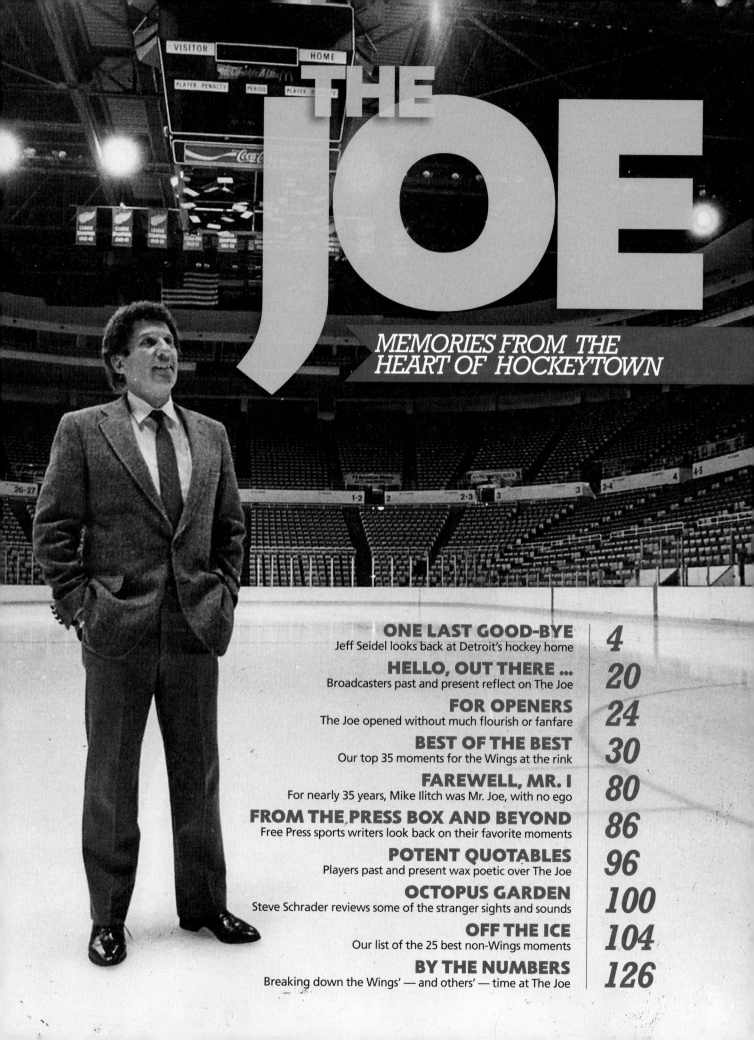

THE JOE

MEMORIES FROM THE HEART OF HOCKEYTOWN

ONE LAST GOOD-BYE
Jeff Seidel looks back at Detroit's hockey home
4

HELLO, OUT THERE ...
Broadcasters past and present reflect on The Joe
20

FOR OPENERS
The Joe opened without much flourish or fanfare
24

BEST OF THE BEST
Our top 35 moments for the Wings at the rink
30

FAREWELL, MR. I
For nearly 35 years, Mike Ilitch was Mr. Joe, with no ego
80

FROM THE PRESS BOX AND BEYOND
Free Press sports writers look back on their favorite moments
86

POTENT QUOTABLES
Players past and present wax poetic over The Joe
96

OCTOPUS GARDEN
Steve Schrader reviews some of the stranger sights and sounds
100

OFF THE ICE
Our list of the 25 best non-Wings moments
104

BY THE NUMBERS
Breaking down the Wings' — and others' — time at The Joe
126

BUILT QUICKLY ON THE CHEAP, THE JOE MAY NEVER HAVE BEEN

GOOD-BYE,

BY JEFF SEIDEL

It's like going to see an old friend, one last time.

Climb the steps to the entrance of Joe Louis Arena. Careful, those steps are steep and can leave you winded.

Through the metal detectors.

Down the concrete concourse — it might be ugly, but it's our ugly.

Take one last look around before the Red Wings move to Little Caesars Arena, a new home that will open in September 2017.

Duck through one of the stiff, red plastic curtains — and the memories and emotions come flooding back.

Suddenly, it is June 7, 1997, and Steve Yzerman, with his missing front tooth, lifts the Stanley Cup — the organization's first in 42 years. The Captain hands the Cup to owner Mike Ilitch as a song blares over the

CONTINUED ON PAGE 7

The long good-bye

On Oct. 17, 2016, the Red Wings turned the rink into a giant darkroom as they opened their final season at Joe Louis Arena before moving to Little Caesars Arena. The Wings beat Ottawa, 5-1, behind Mike Green's hat trick.

NATE SMALLWOOD/DETROIT FREE PRESS

TRULY FINISHED. BUT IT WAS OURS ALONE IN HOCKEYTOWN

OLD FRIEND

Bronze age

Gordie Howe checked out the resemblance when the Red Wings unveiled his statue inside The Joe in April 2007. The statue — 6-feet-4 tall and 12 feet long — was composed of white bronze with integrated glass chips to simulate ice. The artist was Omri Amrany of Highland Park, Ill., who also created the statues of Tigers greats inside Comerica Park, Magic Johnson outside Michigan State's Breslin Center and Michael Jordan outside Chicago's United Center. "Not too many things choke me up," Howe said. "So I guess that's the way of expressing the feelings that I have." Among the attendees for the unveiling were Howe's sons Mark and Marty, former teammates Bill Gadsby and Johnny Wilson, and current Wings Nicklas Lidstrom, Chris Chelios and Kris Draper.
ROMAIN BLANQUART/ DETROIT FREE PRESS

CONTINUED FROM PAGE 4

loudspeakers: "We are the champions, my friends. And we'll keep on fighting 'til the end."

Fighting?

It is March 26, 1997, and Darren Mc-Carty is hammering Colorado's Claude Lemieux — revenge for Lemieux's hit from behind on Kris Draper a year earlier. Sticks and helmets are littered across the ice as Brendan Shanahan intercepts goaltender Patrick Roy. And then, the moment that still lives on YouTube — it can't get any better than this — as Wings goaltender Mike Vernon and Roy lock up, trading punches, knocking the bejesus out of each other. Roy leaves with blood streaming down his face.

Oh, it does get better, in a different way. It is June 13, 2002, and a chant rises through The Joe: "WE WANT THE CUP! WE WANT THE CUP! WE WANT THE CUP!" A horn goes off, and bodies are flying and hearts are soaring and confetti flitters down and the Wings have done it yet again. Yzerman hands the Cup to Scotty Bowman, from a future Hall of Famer to present Hall of Famer, and Bowman skates around the ice in his final moment as a head coach. They all sprawl across the ice for a picture, the Hockey Gods and Mr. I, who raises three fingers. The third Cup since 1997.

This gray, sterile box at 19 Steve Yzerman Drive has hosted it all, from Cups and rock shows to the 1980 Republican presidential nomination of Ronald Reagan to the circus — and by circus, we mean, the biggest, strangest, wackiest moment in figure skating history.

It is Jan. 6, 1994, and Nancy Kerrigan, moments after leaving the practice rink at neighboring Cobo Arena, is sobbing and screaming on the red hallway carpet after being attacked by a large man in a black leather coat and a black hat. She crunches over, holds her knee and cries out, "Why me? Why now?" Two nights later at The Joe, Tonya Harding easily wins the U.S. nationals as Kerrigan watches from a

CONTINUED ON PAGE 8

CONTINUED FROM PAGE 7

skybox. The conspiracy to injure Kerrigan quickly unravels, and Harding eventually pleads guilty to a felony charge.

This is where Al Sobotka, the Zamboni driver, twirled the octopus over his head and Karen Newman sang her heart out, just about every night like clockwork, and everybody joined along with Journey, screaming at the top of their lungs: "Just a city boy, *born and raised in south Detroit.*"

This building is 15-million cubic feet of quirks — the springy boards, the thin, steep steps with the yellow paint, the worn, red plastic chairs, the stairwell that must have come from a giant Erector Set and the shots-on-goal scoreboard that looks like something from a middle-school gymnasium — a seriously old gym.

This building is like an old friend. The one you raised a whole bunch of hell with.

It might be weathered and wrinkled and have a bunch of scars, but it holds your secrets.

And now, it is time to say goodbye.

THE PONTIAC RED WINGS?

When the Wings moved to this arena in December 1979, it was known as "Joe Louis Warehouse" because it was so cold, vast and bleak.

There weren't enough bathrooms. Florescent lightbulbs hung on bare wires in the concourse. Merchandise was sold on card tables. And the team was in disarray under Bruce Norris' ownership.

Nobody seemed happy that the Wings were trading the charm of the Olympia for the coldness of this $34-million building wedged between two expressways, a parking structure, a series of ramps and bridges, and the De-

troit River.

"It really wasn't renovated and ready to go," former Wing Paul Woods recalled. "It didn't make sense. You looked at the two buildings, and we were like, 'Why are we doing this?'"

The players didn't care for it. "We weren't a real happy bunch,"

said Woods, a Detroit left wing in 1977-84 and a Wings radio analyst since 1987.

Joe Louis Arena was named after the famous heavyweight boxer from Detroit, which seems fitting in retrospect, because this place was born out of political

CONTINUED ON PAGE 12

Joe Louis Arena's baby book

Construction started in the spring of 1977 for Detroit's new riverfront sports arena. Although unfinished, Joe Louis Arena opened its the doors on Dec. 12, 1979, for a basketball game between the Michigan Wolverines and the University of Detroit Titans. The Red Wings made their debut 15 days later. Clockwise from the left: 1) Ice covered the Detroit River, but winter's chill didn't stop work on the giant Erector Set rising on its banks. 2) Wings GM Ted Lindsay and Mayor Coleman Young posed for the cameras with an industrial-strength wrench. 3) Only weeks from opening, The Joe still needed plenty of decorating. 4) To many Detroiters, the circular walkway that crossed the Lodge Freeway resembled a Habitrail, and hockey fans were the hamsters scurrying to and fro.
DFP FILE PHOTOS: 1) TONY SPINA. 2) IRA ROSENBERG. 3) TARO YAMASAKI. 4) IRA ROSENBERG

An octopus really can fly

From the catwalk near The Joe's roof, Al the Octopus looked as if he were poised to attack the arena like in some kind of bad science fiction movie. The Joe wasn't packed to the gills because the Red Wings weren't in the house. The fans were watching their out-of-town playoff game on the big screens.

JOHN LUKE/ DETROIT FREE PRESS

CONTINUED FROM PAGE 8

infighting, backdoor battles and a nasty sparring session between the city and the suburbs.

The Wings had played at Olympia Stadium since 1927, at one point finishing first in the league for seven straight years and winning four Stanley Cups in six years at the Old Red Barn on Grand River. Louis had fought there as a young amateur and an old champion; in failing health since the late '70s, he never set foot in The Joe before his death in April 1981.

Detroit Mayor Coleman Young started to construct a 20,000-seat arena on the riverfront in 1977, even though he had no tenants or financing.

Suburban developers tried to lure the Wings to Pontiac next to the Silverdome, offering millions in profit to a franchise that was losing money constantly. The potential Pontiac arena was called Olympia II, and the Wings actually had started selling suites.

The Wings might have ended up in Pontiac if it weren't for an extraordinary meeting between Young and Lincoln Cavalieri, then president of the Wings and Olympia. In a 1989 story published on the 10-year anniversary of The Joe, the Free Press' Chris Christoff provided behind-the-scenes details of their one-on-one meeting in the mayor's office in 1977.

It lasted only an hour or so.

"The first thing Coleman said was, 'I don't want you to move to the cornfields. We want you downtown,'" Cavalieri told the Free Press. "It was quite an experience with the mayor. He didn't screw around. He has a reputation as a hard-nosed guy, but he wanted us down there in the worst way.

"I outlined five or six things we needed. Right there, we agreed on them all. We shook hands. ...

You don't see deals made like that. I didn't think he'd agree."

That single meeting changed everything, the entire face of Detroit, like a pebble hitting the water and creating ripples that continue to this day.

CONTINUED ON PAGE 13

From Olympia to The Joe

On Christmas Eve 1979, the Red Wings practiced in The Joe for the first time. Construction workers paused to watch their hockey heroes. The Wings found the new ice mushy and the plastic-coated boards fast. Arena general manager Lincoln Cavalieri blamed the slow ice on problems with cooling the floor and warm air that blew in an open door.

TARO YAMASAKI/DETROIT FREE PRESS

'I belong to Hockeytown ...'

On the eve of the 1996-97 home opener, Tim Foley of Livonia put the finishing touches of a new logo on the press box. The next night, the Red Wings unveiled "Hockeytown" as their theme for the year and the song "Hey, Hey, Hockeytown." Two decades later, the nickname for Detroit and the song's guitar riffs and refrain remained iconic for the franchise and its fans.

MARY SCHROEDER/DETROIT FREE PRESS

CONTINUED FROM PAGE 12

The Wings reneged on their Pontiac agreement, stayed in Detroit and walked away with a widely criticized sweetheart deal, scooping up all of the profits from The Joe as well as Cobo Arena and a parking garage for 30 years. Which led to Ilitch's grand plan to build an entertainment district in Detroit. Which, in turn, led to the renovation of the Fox Theatre, the construction of Comerica Park and the creation of The District Detroit.

Still, nobody wanted to move out of Olympia.

"Olympia was such a beautiful building with such a great history," Woods said. "The Olympia, in my mind, was a better building. It sounded deep. It had this real intensity. ... I loved going to that place."

When the Wings tried to celebrate 50 years of Norris family ownership on opening night of the 1981-82 season, Bruce Norris was booed vehemently, which he later described as the final straw. He sold everything to Ilitch for

CONTINUED ON PAGE 14

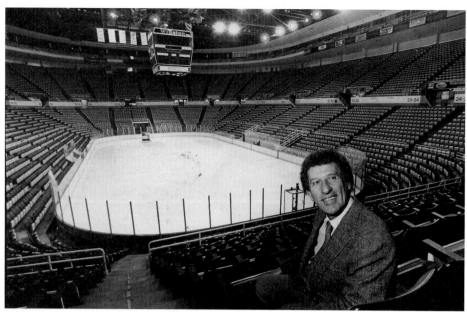

Plenty of pizza, so little pizzazz

When pizza baron Mike Ilitch purchased the Red Wings for $8 million in June 1982, he not only had to improve the product on the ice, he also had to spruce up the building that held the ice. His first victory didn't come until the eighth game. He died Feb. 10, 2017, at age 87.
DETROIT FREE PRESS

CONTINUED FROM PAGE 13

$8 million the following June.

A few weeks shy of his 53rd birthday, Ilitch immediately tried to warm up The Joe by renovating the offices, dressing rooms and press room. He put in new lighting fixtures and ordered paint on the walls. Mirrors were added to the weight room. "So the players can watch their muscles when they work out," coach Nick Polano joked to the Free Press.

A Little Caesars Pizza outlet was built under the stands. Ilitch gave away an American-made car at each home game, trying to lure fans to the arena despite his lousy team and Detroit's struggling auto economy.

On opening night for the 1982-83 season, the fans gave Ilitch a rousing standing ovation. "That was too much; I was all choked up," Ilitch said afterward. "It was a very, very touching thing. Ever see a grown man cry?"

As Ilitch tried to make The Joe less ugly, the really signifi-

cant improvement was how he changed the culture of the entire organization.

"It's my job as leader of the franchise to produce the proper environment," Ilitch told the Free Press in 1982. "This is my way of doing things. I talked it over with my wife and I said, 'Hey, Marian, I can't lay back. I know that we shouldn't do this or we shouldn't do that,' but I said, 'That's me. I've got to go out and aggressively do things the way I do them.' …

"I want to do things that are going to stimulate the fans along with the team members and the staff."

And he kept doing things, right up until his death at age 87 on Feb. 10, 2017.

FROM BOB SEGER TO SERGEI FEDOROV

So take it in one last time.

Look at the banners hanging over the ice; and yes, that sparks another flood of memories. Pow-

CONTINUED ON PAGE 16

A bad case of Cup fever

The tension of a scoreless tie broken, Gerry Todd of Shelby Township whooped it up after Mikael Samuelson's second-period goal in Game 1 of the 2008 Stanley Cup finals against Pittsburgh. Samuelson scored again early in the third period as the Wings won, 4-0. Chris Osgood notched another shutout in Game 2, 3-0, and the Wings eventually won their 11th Stanley Cup in six games.

BRIAN KAUFMAN/DETROIT FREE PRESS

CONTINUED FROM PAGE 14

erful, lump-in-your throat memories. Gordie Howe's visitation and Yzerman's jersey retirement ceremony.

Look at the folks in the stands. The dress code is still hockey casual — jeans and a Wings sweater, the older the better.

Over the years, they have tried to spruce up the concourse with banners, ads, murals, souvenir stands and kiosks, trying to pull a different revenue stream out of every inch of space.

During The Joe's final season, the floor was decorated with the names of the most famous acts to perform there: The Who, Bob Seger, Kid Rock, Madonna and Diana Ross.

But this building always has been about the hockey.

The Russian Five to the Grind Line.

It's Stevie. Shanny. Drapes. Ozzie. Sergei. Vladdie. Probie. Pavel. Z.

The list goes on and on.

This place isn't special because of the steel and concrete.

It's special because of the people and the memories.

It's the players and the ushers and that familiar face checking passes in the parking garage.

"I've been working for the Red Wings for 51 years," said Don Donohue, 81, of Plymouth, who used to be a "gate guy" at a parking lot at the Olympia and had worked almost every night doing the same thing in a booth at the parking garage near The Joe. "I've made up my mind that I'm not going to the new one."

He will retire along with The Joe. "It's time," Donohue said.

Indeed. It's time to say good-bye.

So, cherish the memories from The Joe. The sights and sounds. Hold onto the mental pictures of

CONTINUED ON PAGE 17

THE JOE: GREAT FOR HOCKEY, BAD FOR ARCHITECTURE FANS

Hockey fans will cherish their memories of Joe Louis Arena. Architecture fans not so much.

The gray warehouse-like cladding of the city-owned arena ranked The Joe among the least inspiring public buildings in memory. And the banks of outdoor staircases exposed to the wintry winds off the Detroit River may vie for the least popular architectural feature in town.

But the failures of The Joe do not lie necessarily with its designers, the venerable Detroit firm now known as Smith-GroupJJR, which as always had to make do with budget limitations and other constraints. The biggest drawback rests with the site chosen by city leaders. They placed the arena on the riverfront before we all recognized how important public access to a well-designed waterfront was to urban vitality.

The arena's 1970s-era placement on the riverfront — blocking the views, hemmed in by Cobo Center and moat-like roadways — necessitated an awkward approach through pedestrian bridges and tunnels. This arrangement belied any sense

BY JOHN GALLAGHER

of importance and robbed the arena of those moments of visual climax that culminate in great architecture.

Putting it there was no better than one of those dreary concrete bowls in suburbia surrounded by acres of asphalt — but in this case transferred to the worst possible site on the river.

The future replacement for Joe Louis Arena will no doubt be better. Whether that replacement turns out to be a hotel, a residential tower or whatever, it is inconceivable now that the mistakes of the past could be repeated. Any future replacement will allow the RiverWalk promenade to be extended; it will take full advantage of the river vistas; it will no longer squat fortress-like on the riverbank.

So, shed a nostalgic tear if you will for the many hockey memories at The Joe. But, in terms of architecture, good riddance.

John Gallagher, a business columnist for the Free Press, has covered urban development and architecture for three decades. He is coauthor of "AIA Detroit: The American Institute of Architects Guide to Detroit Architecture," and author of "Great Architecture of Michigan" and "Yamasaki in Detroit: A Search for Serenity," among other books.

CONTINUED FROM PAGE 16

the Stanley Cups and the dazzling players and the rock-'em-sock-'em fights and all of those crazy nights — "Hey, hey, Hockeytown!"

But the building itself?

It was born ugly, and it will die ugly.

So be it. Hockeytown is not a building. It's a story that flows from generation to generation, from Olympia to Little Caesars Arena, and the wonderful stop along the riverfront will live forever.

Stairway to heaven

The notorious 36 concrete steps to enter Joe Louis Arena never looked as inviting as they did for the final home opener in October 2016. Linda and Kevin Smith stopped to admire the artwork and to shoot a photo. When the arena opened in 1979, the Free Press' front-page photo and story focused on "the controversial main entrance." Reginald Ayala, a middle-aged Detroiter, had "no problem whatever, and I'm fat and out of shape," he said after reaching the top.
KIRTHMON F. DOZIER/ DETROIT FREE PRESS

Hail, Little Caesars

Little Caesars Arena, shown in January 2017, was scheduled to be completed by September. Kid Rock, a long-proven hometown draw, was booked for a series of concerts starting Sept. 12 to christen the new home for the Red Wings and the Pistons. In the past two decades, the Romeo-born Rock had played sold-out shows at every major venue in metro Detroit, most recently a 10-night stand at DTE Energy Music Theatre in 2015 for more than 150,000 fans.

ERIC SEALS/DETROIT FREE PRESS

NEW ARENA TO BE STATE OF THE ART; JOE SLATED TO BE DEMOLISHED

BY JC REINDL

Joe Louis Arena's replacement will be a new $635-million arena, situated in a formerly desolate part of Detroit along the old Cass Corridor between downtown and the gentrifying Midtown.

Scheduled to open in September 2017, Little Caesars Arena will be home to the Detroit Red Wings as well as the Detroit Pistons, who will return to the city after a decades-long absence. The Pistons will leave the Palace of Auburn Hills, their home since 1988. Seating capacity for the arena is expected to be around 20,000, essentially the same as at The Joe. There also will be 60 corporate suites.

The Ilitch organization is building Detroit's new arena, with help from about $285 million in public financing. The public financing dollars are from a complex tax-capture arrangement around downtown and the new arena's future commercial footprint, with the state promising to make up any shortfall in school taxes.

The Ilitch organization spent years studying arenas and event centers across the country for ideas for the new venue's design and novel features.

Little Caesars Arena's bowl will feature a flashy exterior "skin" that can change colors, display graphics and show videos. The arena concourse will feature a skylit atrium and be about three times the size of The Joe's concourse, with concessions on one side and restaurants and merchandise shops on the other.

For the hockey players, there will be a below-ground practice rink and training and weight rooms. Practice space for the Pistons is expected to be built apart from the arena but relatively nearby.

Two "gondolas" will hang from the rafters inside the arena, one with seating boxes and party space and the other for media reporters and photographers.

The neighborhood around the arena, once known for its party stores and flophouses, is slated to become home to a new entertainment and residential district. Plans call for hundreds of new apartments, several office buildings and a 350- to 400-room hotel. Most of those buildings will be new construction, although a long-vacant 13-story hotel, The Eddystone, is to be redeveloped into modern housing. A neighboring hotel, the Park Avenue, was demolished in 2015 to make way for the arena's loading dock.

The entire project is called The District Detroit, a 50-block area that also includes Comerica Park, home to the Tigers; Ford Field, home to the Lions; and the Fox Theatre, home to countless concerts and events.

As for The Joe, plans call for demolishing the arena and handing the property to one of Detroit's past creditors to fulfill a deal made during the city's Chapter 9 bankruptcy. That corporation, the Financial Guaranty Insurance Co., could later develop the land with a new hotel, retail stores and riverfront condominiums.

TWO GENERATIONS OF BROADCASTERS REFECT ON TIMES GOOD AND BAD ...

ON THE AIR

BY GEORGE SIPPLE

llogical.

That's what Paul Woods thought as a player when the Red Wings moved from Olympia Stadium to Joe Louis Arena in December 1979.

"It just seemed illogical at the time, but, of course, I wasn't thinking economically back then," said Woods, a Detroit left wing in 1977-84 and a Wings radio analyst since 1987. "It was almost like sick to your stomach when you saw the difference in the two places."

Bruce Martyn, the radio play-by-play announcer in 1964-95, echoed Woods' sentiment that it was far from love at first sight moving from a hockey cathedral to a riverfront warehouse.

"I loved the old Olympia Stadium," said Martyn, a Hockey Hall of Famer. "It was quite a change. The old Olympia was the best seats we ever had to watch a hockey game and broadcast.

"The Joe Louis Arena put us a little father from the ice, but we got used to it in a hurry. We had a nice broadcast area there, our own little booth. Nobody ever bothered us."

Woods said he learned over time to appreciate The Joe.

CONTINUED ON PAGE 22

View from the top

Since 1995, color analyst Paul Woods (left) and play-by-play announcer Ken Kal called Red Wings game for the radio from this perch atop Joe Louis Arena. In the early days, The Joe's 42 rows of seats were criticized as too far from the action. Over the years, broadcasters and writers came to consider their views at The Joe among the best in hockey.

JERRY S. MENDOZA/DETROIT FREE PRESS

VOICES OF THE JOE

The public address announcers for Red Wings games at Joe Louis Arena:

1979-81: John Bell.

1981-84: Mark (Doc) Andrews.

1984-85: Budd Lynch.

1985-86: Lynch and Dave Strader.

1986-88: John Tautges.

1988-2008: Lynch.

2008-11: Lynch and John Fossen.

2011-12: Lynch and Erich Freiny.

2012-17: Freiny.

CONTINUED FROM PAGE 20

"We saw some of the greatest teams and players and coaches ever in the NHL there," he said. "It gathered its own history and became a great place."

Woods said he didn't have a favorite memory, but he did offer up what he considered the greatest stretch in the building's history: the rivalry with the Colorado Avalanche from the middle '90s through the early 2000s. He said four players in particular — Steve Yzerman and Sergei Fedorov for the Wings and Joe Sakic and Peter Forsberg for the Avs — made it memorable.

"All four of them were outstanding in their own right," Woods said. "The level of play was so high. Compete level was so high."

Martyn joked that somewhere on YouTube resided one of his favorite memories, but he didn't go there to watch. He never called a Stanley Cup championship working for the Wings, but he was a guest announcer during the second period of Game 4 in the 1997 Stanley Cup finals. He got to use his signature call: "He shoots ... he S-C-O-O-O-R-E-S!"

"I worked 31 years and never had a Stanley Cup," Martyn said. "When I left them two years later, they did nothing but win

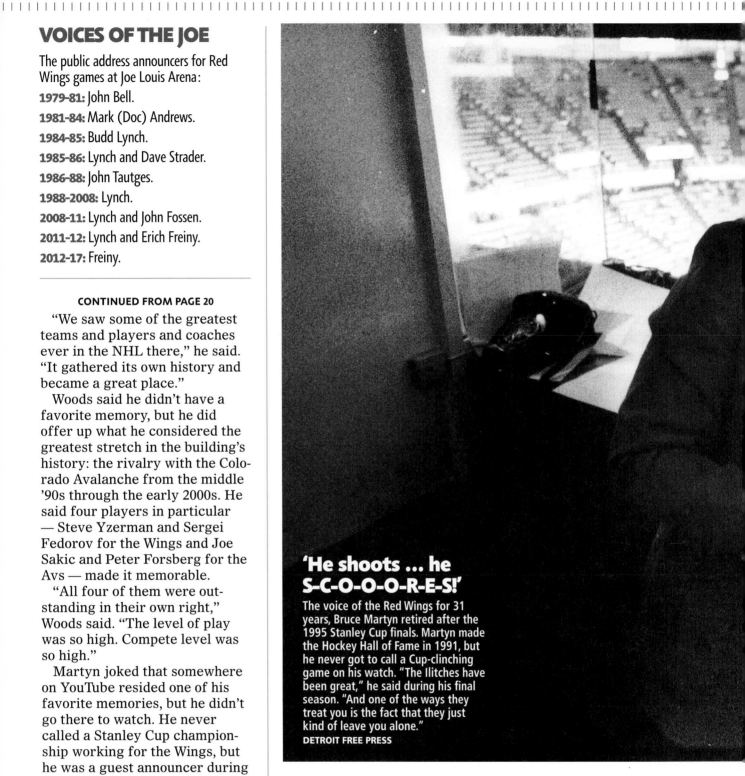

'He shoots ... he S-C-O-O-O-R-E-S!'

The voice of the Red Wings for 31 years, Bruce Martyn retired after the 1995 Stanley Cup finals. Martyn made the Hockey Hall of Fame in 1991, but he never got to call a Cup-clinching game on his watch. "The Ilitches have been great," he said during his final season. "And one of the ways they treat you is the fact that they just kind of leave you alone." **DETROIT FREE PRESS**

Stanley Cups. But Ken Kal was very, very nice and invited me back to the second period of the game against Philadelphia. Darren McCarty scored the goal that won the Stanley Cup for them and I broadcast it, which was pretty exciting for me."

Kal called Martyn one of his idols and they maintained a friendship over the years.

Martyn doesn't get to Wings games much now that he lives in Florida, but he would like to visit Little Caesars Arena.

CONTINUED ON PAGE 23

Two decades together

By whatever iteration — Fox Sports Net, FSN Detroit, FSD, Fox Sports Detroit — Mickey Redmond (left) and Ken Daniels were fixtures at the cable outlet from its 1997 launch.
JULIAN H. GONZALEZ/DETROIT FREE PRESS

BROADCAST TEAMS

The voices of the Red Wings during the Joe Louis Arena era:

ON THE RADIO

1979-86: Bruce Martyn and Sid Abel.

1986-87: Martyn and Mark Champion.

1987-95: Martyn and Paul Woods.

1995-2017: Ken Kal and Woods.

ON TELEVISION

(Some years had more than one broadcast team because two channels televised games.)

1979-80: Martyn/Abel and Larry Osterman/Mickey Redmond.

1980-83: Martyn/Abel and Budd Lynch/Alex Delvecchio.

1983-85: Martyn and Abel.

1985-96: Dave Strader and Redmond.

1996-97: Mike Goldberg and Redmond.

1997-2017: Ken Daniels and Redmond (with fill-ins Pat Verbeek, Larry Murphy, Chris Osgood and Darren Eliot).

CONTINUED FROM PAGE 22

Woods has some mementos from the old rink, but said there's nothing he expected to take from The Joe.

"At my age, it's more the memories you have of the place, what you saw, what you'll reflect on later," he said. "My playing days weren't good at Joe Louis Arena, but what I saw afterwards was. I guess it all turns out good in the end."

Which leads to …

"I guess the biggest question mark for me now is, what history awaits us at the new building?" Woods said. "So many good memories and great memories and great players and coaches. It's all positive now. That makes me excited for the new place as well."

AFTER 52 YEARS OF PRO HOCKEY AT OLYMPIA STADIUM ON GRAND RIVER, A NEW DOWNTOWN HOME FOR THE DETROIT

A GRAND

BY BILL MCGRAW AND CHARLIE VINCENT

Late in the second period, Red Wings forward Glenn Hicks and Blues defenseman Bryan Maxwell were sent off for conducting the first hockey bout in the new arena named for the former heavyweight champion who grew up in Detroit.

The 19,742 fans for the first game at Joe Louis Arena — who let out a chorus of boos each time the announcer mentioned the riverfront building's name — had to wait only another 136 seconds for the evening's second fight, which featured Detroit's Pete Mahovlich and St. Louis' Wayne Babych.

Alas, Wings fans would need to wait much longer for their team's first victory in its new $34-million home. Two goals 2½ minutes apart in the third period — each with future Hall of Famer Bernie Federko as a central figure — gave the Blues a 3-2 victory. The Wings entered the game tied with Hartford for the Norris Division dungeon.

"I thought it was the night we would start a new era," Wings coach Bobby Kromm said.

"I'm disappointed," general manager Ted Lindsay said. "We gave it away. It's sad for all the loyal fans. They were ready to raise the roof off the new building."

The differences between Joe Louis Arena — called "Louis Arena" on second reference in newspaper stories — and the Olympia — the Old Red Barn that was home to the professional hockey franchise for 52 years — were striking for players and fans alike.

CONTINUED ON PAGE 26

Home sweet home?

The 19,742 fans who saw the Red Wings' first game at Joe Louis Arena paid $11, $10, $9 or $7. Those prices were among the reasons fans gave the arena mixed reviews. Tickets were $3 higher than at Olympia. A $10 ticket in 1979 would cost about $35 these days. The Wings lost that night to St. Louis, a harbinger of the terrible things to come. That season, they were 6-4-2 at Olympia but 8-17-3 at The Joe, including an 0-5-2 home stand in February.

ALAN R. KAMUDA/DETROIT FREE PRESS

RED WINGS OPENED ON THE DETROIT RIVER ON DEC. 27, 1979.
THE KEY POINTS FROM FREE PRESS COVERAGE AT THE TIME:

OPENING

FOR OPENERS

By the numbers for the first game at Joe Louis Arena, a 3-2 Red Wings loss to the Blues on Dec. 27, 1979:

19,742

Fans at the game, breaking the team record of 16,678 set at the Olympia in a 4-1 loss to Montreal on Nov. 1, 1978.

9:55

Time left in the first period when St. Louis left wing Brian Sutter scored the first goal in The Joe.

18:17

Time left in the second period when rookie center Dennis Sobchuk scored the Wings' first goal.

2:25

Span in the third period in which the Blues turned a 2-1 deficit into a 3-2 advantage, on a goal and an assist by Bernie Federko, who would finish his Hall of Fame career with one season in Detroit.

29-25

Shots-on-goal edge by the Wings.

CONTINUED FROM PAGE 24

First-night fans found a spacious arena dominated by reds and grays. There were no pillars to block their sight, but also no balconies like the $7 mezzanine at the 14,200-seat Olympia. The sides of The Joe rose more gradually than at Olympia, and fans in the distant, middle sections of the 42-row banks were nearly 20 yards farther from the action than they were at Olympia.

Ticket prices were $3 higher in the new arena. They sold for $11, $10, $9 and $7. About 200 executive box-level seats were to go for $15, but that level wasn't finished yet.

Earlier in the week, the Wings had skated in their new home and found the ice mushy and the boards fast. The boards were coated with plastic; Olympia's were wooden.

After the opener, the arena ice again was a matter of discussion. Nearly everyone agreed it was soft and slow, unlike Olympia's hard and fast surface, and some players said it caused teammates to bobble normally easy-to-handle passes.

But no one blamed the loss on the frozen water. "They played on the same ice, too," said Wings rookie Mike Foligno, who still managed to wheel around.

The standing-room-only crowd easily topped the Olympia attendance record of 16,678 set in 1978. It was a bit shy of the NHL record of 20,009, set in St. Louis in 1973.

Despite the extra fans, the noise level seemed lower than at Olympia, whose compact confines kept screams, smoke and on-ice action close to the crowd.

"It was strange," Kromm said. "We looked at it like a road game."

Left wing Errol Thompson said: "It's a beautiful building, but more of a far-away crowd."

Fans gave Louis Arena mixed reviews.

"This is too large," said Clair Sass of Detroit, who had owned season tickets for 27 years. "We don't hear the puck, we don't hear the sticks, nothing. But you can see OK as long as people don't walk up and down the aisles."

"At first it seemed a lot bigger, but as the game goes on, it's a lot easier to follow things," said Peggy O'Connor of Grosse Pointe Woods, a season-ticket holder for three years. "It'll be better than Olympia."

"It's beautiful," said Bill Fondaro of Dearborn, an usher at Tiger Stadium. "Looking around, it seems no one has a bad seat, and once they get organized and learn how to clear the aisles and things, it's going to be great. But I miss the Barn."

"The view's terrific," said Vaughn Derderian of Southfield. "We're further away than last season, but the view is better."

Restroom lines were a bane for fans. So were concession stand lines, largely because fans had to get in a separate line for each item they wanted to purchase: one line for popcorn, another for soft drinks, yet another for hot dogs.

With the Wings up, 2-1, in the third period, Federko took a pass from the corner to the right of goalie Rogie Vachon and slipped the puck into the net at 11:16. With Wings defenseman Barry Long in the penalty box for interference, Federko helped set up the decisive goal, which came when Blair Chapman jammed the puck, trapped by Vachon, through the netminder's legs at 13:41.

"That guy kind of surprised me, coming from behind the net," Vachon explained.

The Wings outshot the Blues, 29-25, and had numerous scoring chances. "But you got to bury it," Kromm said.

St. Louis left wing Brian Sutter became the first player to score a goal in the sparkling new sports emporium when he beat Vachon with a backhand at short range midway through the first period.

The Wings tied the game at 1:43 of the second period, thanks to Foligno, who skated in with the puck and faked a shot before sliding a pass across the goalmouth to Dennis Sobchuk, who slapped it in.

Dan Bolduc made it 2-1 for the Wings late in the period by netting a loose puck in front of goalie Mike Liut while both teams were a man short.

Kromm and Lindsay each said they had hoped for more production from their two top lines — Dale McCourt, Vaclav Nedomansky, Dan Labraaten, Foligno, Mahovlich and Thompson.

AN UNLIKELY FIRST VICTORY

The Red Wings that moved into Joe Louis Arena in late December 1979 were not a very good team.

They would finish last in the Norris Division at 26-43-11, missing a playoff berth by 10 points. Only three teams — the Quebec Nordiques, Winnipeg Jets and Colorado Rockies — notched fewer points than the Wings' 63 points.

But, somehow, the Wings won three of their four meetings with the New York Islanders, who would win their first of four straight Stanley Cups. Even better, the Wings' first victory at The Joe came at expense of the Isles before 18,101 fans.

On Dec. 30, three nights after the opening 3-2 loss to St. Louis, the Wings stunned the Islanders, 4-2. Detroit scored four times in the game's first 13 minutes against Glenn (Chico) Resch: Dan Labraaten at 1:47, Dan Bolduc at 4:56, Errol Thompson at 8:57 and Vaclav Nedomansky at 13:17.

New York's goals, by Bryan Trottier and Anders Kallur, came late in the second period. Rogie Vachon stopped 30 shots, including flurries at the end of the second and third periods, to earn the game's first star.

Not as bad as it looks

Defenseman Jean Hamel ran into nothing but bad luck right after the Red Wings moved from Olympia to The Joe. On New Year's Eve 1979, he suffered a concussion against the Colorado Rockies and missed several games. On Jan. 16, again against the Rockies, he suffered a back injury by crashing into the boards 20 seconds after the puck dropped. He had been checking Lanny McDonald. As was the custom at the time, his teammates (including Dennis Polonich, Mike Foligno and Paul Woods) carried him off the ice for additional treatment. Hamel went straight to Detroit Osteopathic Hospital. The diagnosis: Broken tailbone, out 4-6 weeks. Only 13,273 fans saw the Wings beat the Rockies, 5-1.
HUGH GRANNUM/DETROIT FREE PRESS

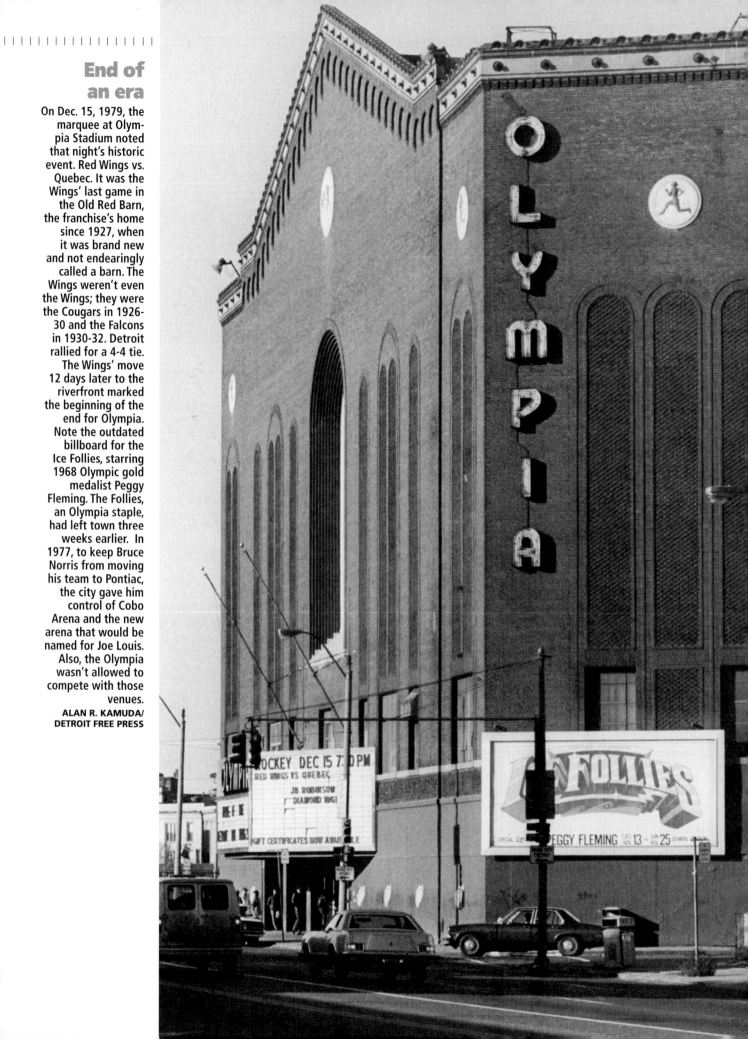

End of an era

On Dec. 15, 1979, the marquee at Olympia Stadium noted that night's historic event. Red Wings vs. Quebec. It was the Wings' last game in the Old Red Barn, the franchise's home since 1927, when it was brand new and not endearingly called a barn. The Wings weren't even the Wings; they were the Cougars in 1926-30 and the Falcons in 1930-32. Detroit rallied for a 4-4 tie. The Wings' move 12 days later to the riverfront marked the beginning of the end for Olympia. Note the outdated billboard for the Ice Follies, starring 1968 Olympic gold medalist Peggy Fleming. The Follies, an Olympia staple, had left town three weeks earlier. In 1977, to keep Bruce Norris from moving his team to Pontiac, the city gave him control of Cobo Arena and the new arena that would be named for Joe Louis. Also, the Olympia wasn't allowed to compete with those venues.

**ALAN R. KAMUDA/
DETROIT FREE PRESS**

GOOD-BYE, OLD BARN

Beatlemania

Four lads from Liverpool played an Olympia doubleheader on Sept. 6, 1964, during their first U.S. tour and the height of Beatlemania. "A Hard Day's Night," the Beatles' first movie, had opened the previous week at 14 neighborhood theaters, noted the Detroit Daily Press. (A strike had silenced the Free Press and Detroit News.) Introducing … the Beatles (clockwise from top left): Paul McCartney, Ringo Starr, John Lennon and George Harrison. Their 12-song set: "Twist And Shout," "You Can't Do That," "All My Loving," "She Loves You," "Things We Said Today," "Roll Over Beethoven," "Can't Buy Me Love," "If I Fell," "I Want to Hold Your Hand," "Boys," "A Hard Day's Night" and "Long Tall Sally." The Beatles performed another Olympia doubleheader in 1966.

TONY SPINA/DETROIT FREE PRESS

The fans came to the 1,790th and final NHL contest at Olympia Stadium armed with banners (such as "Thanks for 7 Cups and 52 years of memories"), boat horns, toilet paper, eggs and a fish. Much of the garbage ended up on the ice during the game on Dec. 15, 1979, delaying play many times.

The 15,609 fans stood several deep in every nook and cranny. They arrived early, took pictures and swapped memories of great games past. They lingered after the game, booed the mention of Joe Louis Arena and listened to the organist play "Auld Lang Syne."

And thanks to a frantic final frame, the Red Wings didn't lose their finale in the Old Red Barn. Only with a 20-2 edge in shots and goals by Errol Thompson at 6:58, Vaclav Nedomansky at 7:44 and Greg Joly at 18:35 did the Wings manage a 4-4 tie with the lowly Quebec Nordiques.

Olympia opened Oct. 15, 1927, with a rodeo, an eight-day promotion that lost money. Hockey debuted Nov. 22, 1927, when the Stanley Cup champion Ottawa Senators beat the hometown Cougars, 2-1. Herbert Hoover and the Black Muslims held rallies there. Joe Louis boxed there as a young amateur and as an old champion. Customers paid to see the rise of welterweight Thomas Hearns and the decline of heavyweight Elvis Presley who, shortly before his death, sang lethargic 30-second versions of his old hits. There were better concerts: Elvis in 1957, the Beatles in 1964, the Rolling Stones in 1969, Frank Sinatra in 1976 and countless more.

On Grand River at McGraw, the red-brick Olympia stood four stories high, a city block wide and another block long. An old-timers game filled the Olympia one final time on Feb. 21, 1980, when the 1979-80 Wings beat an alumni team, 6-2. Fans booed when the last-place Wings scored; their heroes of yesteryear received numerous standing ovations. Gordie Howe, in his final pro season, back in the NHL with the Hartford Whalers and a month from his 52nd birthday, scored the building's final goal. "It was a fitting way to see the Old Barn close," he said. "The fans were great as always."

On July 9, 1986, a wrecking crew started dismantling the building. The site supervisor was Jim Martin, a Lions star during their championship years in the 1950s. As fans dropped by to take pictures and carry off bricks, Martin summed up the end of an era: "This place is as close to me as it is to most people in this town. … Now all that's left are the memories. It's all pretty depressing."

IN NEARLY FOUR DECADES AT THE JOE, THE RED WINGS CONTINUALLY RAISED EXPECTATIONS — ALONG WITH RAISING FOUR STANLEY CUP BANNERS AND SEVEN RETIRED NUMBERS

WINGED WONDER

FROM FREE PRESS STAFF OVER THE DECADES; EDITED BY GENE MYERS

NO. 1: JUNE 7, 1997

HOCKEYTOWN BECOMES STANLEYTOWN

AFTER 42 YEARS OF FUTILITY, CUP RETURNS TO MOTOR CITY — AND RIDES IN CAPTAIN'S PORSCHE

With a Game 7 victory at Olympia on April 14, 1955, the Red Wings not only earned the Stanley Cup, but they also recieved handshakes from the Montreal Canadiens.

"They relished it just as keenly as they had the spectacular 3-1 Detroit triumph which set the stage," Marshall Dann wrote for the Free Press.

Why? What made the traditional hockey handshake such a big deal?

Well, it was a different time for the sport everywhere and a different hockey landscape in the Motor City. By 1955, with Gordie Howe scoring and Terry Sawchuk stopping, Detroit expected ultimate victory each spring. The Wings had won "seven straight National League titles," which was how the Free Press described finishing first in the regular season, which carried a lot more cache with players and fans in the '50s than it does today. Also, the Wings had won four Stanley Cups over the same span.

In 1955, the Wings finished two points ahead of the Canadiens and captured the Cup by beating Montreal in seven games. A goal by Howe, sandwiched between two by Alex Delvecchio, was the official Cup winner.

In 1954, the Wings finished seven points ahead of the Canadiens and captured the Cup by beating Montreal in seven games. A goal by Tony Leswick, after 4:29 of OT, was the Cup winner.

But after the 1954 series, the Canadiens refused to shake hands. The Wings felt snubbed. "The Canadiens stunned all of Canada," the Free Press wrote, "by failing to make the customary sportsmanlike maneuver."

But after the 1955 series it was a different story. According to the Free Press, "Tom Johnson, a fierce competitor, led the rush to congratulate the Wings. Captain Butch Bouchard was close behind. The Detroiters heartily returned those handshakes. They knew they'd been through a tough one."

With their seventh Stanley Cup, the Wings tied Montreal and Toronto for the most in NHL history.

Fast forward 42 years to Joe Louis Arena on the Detroit riverfront. Not only hadn't the Wings won their eighth Cup, most of those years they had no realistic shot of doing so. And when they were good, they couldn't finish. Six times they reached the final series ('56, '61, '63, '64, '66, '95); only in 1964 did they play a game in which a Detroit victory meant the Cup. That year, the Wings lost Game 6 when Toronto's Bob Baun, despite a broken ankle from a Howe shot, scored in overtime and were routed in Game 7

CONTINUED ON PAGE 31

Blades of glory

Near the boards, owners Mike and Marian Ilitch thanked coach Scotty Bowman, who had ditched his suit and tie to don his skates so that he could take the Stanley Cup for a lap. "I have always dreamt about doing that," Bowman said. "I always wanted to be a player in the NHL and skate with the Cup."

JULIAN H. GONZALEZ/DETROIT FREE PRESS

CONTINUED FROM PAGE 30

at Olympia, 4-0.

In the 1990s, the Wings turned into an NHL powerhouse again, but each spring brought more heartache. By 1997, the Wings had lost three times in the first round, once in the second, once in the conference finals and once in the championship series, a sweep by the New Jersey Devils. The 1996 Wings even had won 62 games, a record, but lost to Colorado, 4-2, in the conference finals.

In the 1997 playoffs, the Wings eliminated St. Louis in six games, Anaheim in four and Colorado in six. Only the Avalanche series had ended at The Joe.

In the Stanley Cup finals, the Wings won Games 1 and 2 in Philadelphia by 4-2 scores. Then came a 6-1 blowout at The Joe.

And 42 years of frustration finally lifted at 10:50 on a Saturday night. With the Flyers defeated, 2-1, the horn blew, the confetti fell and the fireworks went off — famously startling coach Scotty Bowman, already wearing his Stanley Cup champions cap.

Helmets, gloves, sticks and pads went skyward and scattered all over the rink. The bench emptied and a mass of Wings engulfed goalie Mike Vernon, the Conn Smythe winner as playoff MVP.

The Stanley Cup went to the captain, Steve Yzerman, and eventually to every Wing, even owner Mike Ilitch.

"I don't know how to describe it," Yzerman said. "I'm glad the game is over, but I wish it never ended."

At 3:15 a.m., Yzerman emerged from The Joe with the Cup held above his head and somehow squeezed it into the backseat of his Porsche. He drove off as a handful of celebrating fans cheered. For everyone, 42 years in the hockey wilderness was 41 years too long.

Love that smile

Always a good-looking guy, Steve Yzerman wasn't thrilled with his gap-toothed smile in his most iconic photos. He suffered an infected tooth late in the season, had it removed in the second round and didn't have time for a replacement before the finals. "Good timing, eh?" he said. "Here I am, looking like a hillbilly. Not that there's anything wrong with that."

MARY SCHROEDER/DETROIT FREE PRESS

BRINGING THE STANLEY CUP BACK TO DETROIT WAS A HEALING MOMENT FOR ALL

How the Free Press' award-winning columnist and best-selling author covered the events of June 7, 1997, at The Joe:

BY MITCH ALBOM

The crowd was thinning and the noise was dying down. The champagne showers had turned his hair into a sticky nest. Steve Yzerman glanced over the messy remains of the Red Wings' locker room, then told a story.

He had been in Las Vegas a few years back. He was sitting at a craps table. Two guys from Windsor, Ontario, recognized him and made the typical fuss. *Hey, it's Yzerman from the Red Wings!* Then they looked at the gambling action, looked at The Captain, and one of them whispered, "We better get away from here. There's no luck at this table."

Yzerman "wanted to slug 'em," he recalled.

He didn't, of course. He suffered silently, which is how we do it around Detroit, and the sting of that insult and all the others like it bore deep inside his stomach, churned around like a sleepless wasp, year after year — until one night in June 1997. Until that moment when the final horn sounded and Yzerman threw his stick and his curses to the wind and he lifted off toward the open arms of goalie Mike Vernon as a thundering roar shook Joe Louis Arena and you know what? The heck with those guys from Windsor — the whole *world* wanted to be around Steve Yzerman now.

A wounded deer leaps the highest, that's what they say. And if the Wings' soaring championship had one common theme it was this: Heal the wounds, mend the tear, end the suffering and leap into salvation. This was not a championship in a city, it was a championship for a city, a city that had waited 42 years for hockey recognition and was still waiting, thank you, for the non-hockey kind.

Nearly everyone brought some sort of long wait, personal scar or sad history into the Stanley Cup playoffs.

And, as if filled with healing waters, the Cup made them all better.

LONG TIME COMING

There was of course, Yzerman, the 32-year-old captain, who had been working down by the Detroit River since Ronald Reagan's first term. He finally admitted in an emotional moment hours after the Wings won the Cup by beating Philadelphia, 2-1, that the whispers all these years had stung him, even if he never showed it.

"They always say, 'He's a good player but he didn't win it,'" Yzerman said. "And now they can't say that anymore. No matter what, they can't say it, you know? These past five years, there were summers where I didn't even want to go outside. I didn't want to be recognized, I put on my hat, my sunglasses, I walked around in a shell. You're embarrassed. I've felt that way before."

He flicked a champagne drop off his nose. No more embarrassment.

Healed by the Cup.

And how about The Mother of All Facial Hair Growers — Brendan Shanahan? He began the year in Hartford, wondering whether his career was destined to end in oblivion. And there he was kissing the Cup like a long-lost friend.

"Does it match your dream of what it would be like?" I asked Shanahan hours later, as he dashed behind a curtain for another photo with the trophy.

CONTINUED ON PAGE 33

A man of the people

During the celebration, Darren McCarty decided to climb the penalty box — an area he knew well from his physical play — to give fans a special salute. In the locker room, McCarty declared: "They can shove that '1955.' Now it's '97. … Now it's glory time, baby!"

MARY SCHROEDER/DETROIT FREE PRESS

CONTINUED FROM PAGE 32

"Match it? It exceeds it!" he gushed. "I want to do it again!"

Healed by the Cup.

THE GLORY OF THEIR TIMES

There was the sacrifice behind every set of hands that held that chalice and skated around The Joe's ice. There was Vernon, ready to sell his house a few months ago because he knew he was going to be traded, and now here he was, the Conn Smythe Trophy winner, the most valuable player of the playoffs.

There was Sergei Fedorov, who swallowed his late-season demotion to defenseman and dug inside himself, discovering his own way back to the star he was supposed to be.

There was Joe Kocur, who was out of hockey altogether, his knuckles a bruised mess. Heck, he was playing in recreational leagues less than six months ago. "The lowest moment," he admitted, "was when a guy came on the radio and said the rumor isn't true, Detroit wasn't going to sign me. I heard that and thought, 'That's it. It's over.'"

But here he was holding a cigar. It's never over, as long as you dream.

Healed by the Cup.

There was Darren McCarty, who fought through personal problems to become the gritty core of this team. When he scored the winning goal against the Flyers — on a dipsy-doodle move so unlike him it had to be heaven-sent — the Wings on the bench jumped so high I thought someone juiced 1,000 volts through their rear ends.

And how about McCarty's best buddy, Kris Draper? Last year at this time, his face was swollen and his jaw was wired shut and he was drinking soup and milkshakes, because Claude Lemieux cheap-shotted him in the final game of the failed Western Conference finals. More than any single moment, that blow created a purpose for this year's team.

And more than any single moment, the vengeful beating of Lemieux on March 26 convinced this team that no opponent could contain its spirit.

Now here was Draper, one year after the incident, cigar in teeth, jaw intact, nothing on his chin but the bushy red goatee.

"I don't even remember last

CONTINUED ON PAGE 35

THE CAPTAIN'S HANDOFF WAS HEARD 'ROUND THE WORLD

BY KEITH GAVE

The image of Steve Yzerman skating around the ice, the Stanley Cup over his head as he flashed that beautiful gap-toothed grin that told the world, "I am a hockey player and this is my dream," represented the most iconic event in The Joe's history, because it was our dream, too. But it's what The Captain did after briefly handing the Cup to owner Mike Ilitch that stands as one of hockey's biggest moments.

Hockey purists understand they can learn a lot about a club by what a captain does with the Cup when he has finished his waltz. Yzerman scanned his jubilant teammates until his eyes landed on the oldest man on the team. Yzerman skated a few strides and handed the Cup to Viacheslav (Slava) Fetisov, the 39-year-old legendary Soviet Red Army defenseman who was ending his career in Detroit.

"You don't think this way, you know, like who's going to be next. You're just so happy," Fetisov said nearly two decades later. "And when the captain — *my captain* — he gave the Cup to me, it was … not describable."

Before taking his lap around the rink, though, Fetisov sought his Russian comrade, center Igor Larionov.

"I'm thinking, 'Instead of going around by myself, maybe we can share this moment together,'" Fetisov recalled. "So I said, 'Igor, let's go.'"

And they did.

"I'd never seen two people holding the Cup like that and skating together," left wing Brendan Shanahan said. "They were so excited. … It was just a perfect moment."

And a meaningful one, too, added defenseman Nicklas Lidstrom, a Swede who had heard many denigrating rumors about Europeans in the NHL.

"Stevie really showed the respect he had for the Russians," Lidstrom said, "and I think it was a perfect fit that they skated the Cup together, Slava and Igor. They broke a barrier from where they came. …

"And I think it showed the camaraderie of a team, where you accept the Europeans and you accept the Russians — and they're a big part of your team. That really shows when your captain is handing off the Stanley Cup off to two Russians that meant so much to our team."

That's precisely what Yzerman had in mind. He had heard for too long from too many people that all those Europeans — all those Russians, in particular — were precisely why the Wings would never reach the summit. Detroit also featured Russian forwards Sergei Fedorov and Slava Koslov and defenseman Vladimir Konstantinov. With Fetisov and Larionov, they were called the Russian Five, and they often played as a unit.

"This is what's wrong with your team: You're never going to win with the Russian players," Yzerman said of those warnings. "And we're all like, 'You don't know these guys. *You don't know these guys!*'

"Slava and Igor, these guys were really admired and respected by not just the other Russian players, but by all our guys. They were really popular guys, they were unique personalities. They were very proud of their Russian heritage and really proud of what they've accomplished. And they also really wanted to win the Stanley Cup, there was no questioning that. They were great teammates, well-respected veterans on our team, and we all loved them. They deserved that moment."

Larionov described winning the Stanley Cup and skating with it alongside Fetisov as part of "the greatest day of my life.

"That was really special for us, and very, very good of Stevie doing this for two old Russians, you know?" he said. "Everybody who believes that the Russians are not good enough, not tough enough to win the Cup, we heard all of this. So it was amazing when we get the Cup and skate around the rink with 20,000 fans. That was a very nice feeling."

Validating the European/Russian influence, as Yzerman did with that iconic handoff, had

CONTINUED ON PAGE 35

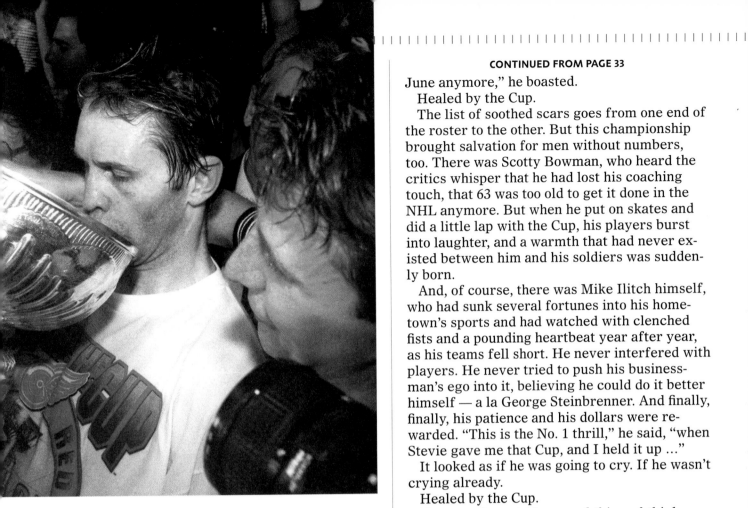

CONTINUED FROM PAGE 33

June anymore," he boasted.

Healed by the Cup.

The list of soothed scars goes from one end of the roster to the other. But this championship brought salvation for men without numbers, too. There was Scotty Bowman, who heard the critics whisper that he had lost his coaching touch, that 63 was too old to get it done in the NHL anymore. But when he put on skates and did a little lap with the Cup, his players burst into laughter, and a warmth that had never existed between him and his soldiers was suddenly born.

And, of course, there was Mike Ilitch himself, who had sunk several fortunes into his hometown's sports and had watched with clenched fists and a pounding heartbeat year after year, as his teams fell short. He never interfered with players. He never tried to push his businessman's ego into it, believing he could do it better himself — a la George Steinbrenner. And finally, finally, his patience and his dollars were rewarded. "This is the No. 1 thrill," he said, "when Stevie gave me that Cup, and I held it up …"

It looked as if he was going to cry. If he wasn't crying already.

Healed by the Cup.

Now, maybe outsiders read this and think, "What sentimental drivel." Well, that's why they're outsiders. They don't understand what hockey means to this town — more importantly, what pride and camaraderie and unity of spirit mean to this town.

"We've had some disappointments and we've broken people's hearts," Yzerman said, "but everybody kept coming back. They kept coming back. They kept coming back, every year, and cheering louder."

Strike up the band. No more whispers at the craps table, no more watching Gretzky or Messier with envy. No more Claude Lemieux, no more Patrick Roy, no more ghosts of San Jose, Toronto, St. Louis or anybody else. It's Detroit, now. Detroit. There's a giant 25-foot chalice on our City-County Building, there's a parade and there's a snapshot in my mind, your mind and the mind of the man, woman or child sitting next to you as you read this. It's the snapshot of Yzerman and his long-awaited smile, hoisting that trophy high into goose-bump land. It pulls us together, that snapshot, and better yet, it always will. They shoot, we soar. Silver threads and golden needles could not mend more than this Cup.

CONTINUED FROM PAGE 34

far-reaching implications for the National Hockey League, too.

"That was recognition from a North American captain to two Russians saying, 'Hey, without you two guys, your play, without your leadership, we wouldn't have done this,'" said Jim Devellano, the Wings' senior vice president. "But you have to remember, too, a few years back when under (NHL president) John Ziegler we decided we were going to expand the footprint of the league across the USA, going from a 21-team league to 30.

"That's a big expansion, and it could have never, ever been accomplished without European-born players. I knew what the player personnel was like across the league, and we needed the Europeans to come over here to make us a strong, 30-team league. And the Russians did it big-time."

Happier times

The muscle of the Wings' defense, Vladimir Konstantinov sipped champagne in the victorious locker room. Six days later, after a team party that ended a week of celebrations and marked the start of the off-season, a limousine carrying defenseman Slava Fetisov, team masseur Sergei Mnatsakanov and Konstantinov crashed in Birmingham. Mnatsakanov's left side and both legs were paralyzed. Konstantinov remained in a coma for more than month with a brain injury. He eventually regained the ability to speak and to walk, but he was never the same mentally or physically.

JULIAN H. GONZALEZ/ DETROIT FREE PRESS

A DISH BEST SERVED COLD
VENGEANCE AT LAST FOR LEMIEUX'S CHEAP SHOT

There was a hockey game to played, to be won on this wild night. But the Wings took care of some old business first.

It started with a scrum late in the first period, and the Wings started pairing off with Colorado players. Lo and behold, Darren McCarty found a dance partner in Claude Lemieux, who mangled Kris Draper's face 10 months earlier with a check from behind. And, to this day, Lemieux had shown no remorse for it.

"I guess it was a payback," McCarty said. "An opportunity presented itself, and something happened."

"Something" was a bloody pummeling of Lemieux, Public Enemy No. 1 in Hockeytown. McCarty started the tango when he spun away from a linesman and coldcocked Lemieux. Lemieux fell to his knees, fans jump to their feet and it was Fight Night at The Joe. Ten minutes of brawling followed.

On the undercard, pitting the goalies, Mike Vernon blooded Patrick Roy and wrestled him to the ice. Igor Larionov fought Peter Forsberg. But the main event always was going to be McCarty-Lemieux.

McCarty whacked Lemieux again with a left, and when Lemieux assumed the turtle position on the ice while holding his bleeding face, McCarty held him by the back of the neck with one hand and pummeled him with the other, throwing punches that appeared to have the force of the entire, roaring building behind them.

Before he was finished, McCarty dragged Lemieux, stunned and bloody, to the Wings' bench, where Draper watched.

"Mac is such a team guy and he wanted to stick up for me," Draper said. "I consider us best friends, and I was happy he did what he did for me."

So it was over — the Lemieux affair? Yes, Draper said, and that left only a game to be decided.

Between the fights and pileups that continued for two periods, when there wasn't blood on the ice and players exchanging blows, on the rare occasions there wasn't chaos, there was hockey. It was in those moments that the Wings showed they could beat — as well as beat up — the defending Stanley Cup champions.

The Wings showed guts, skill and resilience to erase a two-goal, third-period deficit for a 6-5 victory on an overtime goal by, who else, McCarty.

"That's one to remember," McCarty said. "We stuck together in all aspects of our game. That's old-time hockey. That's fun stuff."

McCarty's goal 39 seconds into overtime ended Colorado's four-game winning streak over the Wings.

"When you go through war," McCarty said, "sometimes you need a little feistiness. To see Vernie in there slugging away, that's great."

Afterward, the Avalanche coaches and players were incensed. Coach Marc Crawford even elbowed defenseman Aaron Ward and tried to barge into the officials' dressing room. "That team has no heart," alternate captain Mike Keane said. "Detroit had the opportunity to do that in our building, but they didn't. … Everyone is gutless on that team, and I'd love to see them in the playoffs."

That happened, of course, and the Wings won in six games. The next round of bloodshed came Nov. 11, 1997, at The Joe. Lemieux answered the talk around the NHL, and maybe on his team, about his suspect character because of his cheap shot on Draper and submissiveness against McCarty.

At the opening face-off, Lemieux whacked McCarty across his chest with a right fist. A fight ensued, a real fight this time, with Lemieux squaring off instead of retreating into his shell like a turtle.

"I'm not going to have a bodyguard," Lemieux said later. "I can take care of myself."

Lemieux stood up to McCarty, even after McCarty reached over with his left hand to pry off Lemieux's helmet and protective shield. They exchanged air punches until McCarty switched to his right, landed two jabs and then connected with a haymaker of a left hook.

When McCarty wrestled Lemieux to the ice, there arose the loudest cheer at The Joe since June when the Wings won the Cup.

"I respect him for doing that as a hockey player," McCarty said. "But I still have no respect for him as a human being. He still hasn't apologized to Draper for what he did."

Colorado won the game, 2-0. Lemieux had proven his courage (or stupidity), but Public Enemy No. 1 also left town with a big mouse under his right eye.

Voice of the turtle

Colorado's Claude Lemieux turtled when he took this beating from Darren McCarty in March 1997. Lemieux started their rematch in November 1997, tried going toe-to-toe with his foe and suffered another beating. "I'm not going to have a bodyguard," he declared.

JULIAN H. GONZALEZ/DETROIT FREE PRESS

NO. 3:
JUNE 13, 2002

HOCKEY GODS

HALL OF FAMERS SEND RETIRING BOWMAN OUT A CHAMPION

The final horn sounded, the confetti fell, and as the Red Wings celebrated their 3-1 victory over Carolina that brought them the Stanley Cup, coach Scotty Bowman skated onto the ice. He found owner Mike Ilitch amid the throng, hugged him and whispered something in his ear.

"What he said in my ear was, 'Mike, it's time. The time is right now,'" Ilitch said. "'It's time to go.'"

And so, after three Cups in six seasons, after a record nine Cups as coach, after setting every other coaching record there was to set, Bowman skated off into the sunset. When NHL commissioner Gary Bettman handed the Stanley Cup to captain Steve Yzerman, Yzerman handed it right to Bowman, and Bowman took a victory lap around the ice, holding it high.

"What a way for the greatest coach in the history of the sport to exit," general manager Ken Holland said.

After three straight disappointing playoffs, the Wings added three potential Hall of Famers over the summer: Dominik Hasek, Brett Hull and Luc Robitaille. That gave them nine — and intense pressure to win the Cup or else.

"He did an incredible job with all these egos and high-profile players," Holland said. "He got them all to buy into the team concept. He's the master. It's a team that I'll never forget, and I'm sure a lot of fans will never forget."

Bowman, 68, said he decided to retire over the Olympic break in February. He told maybe a few people he trusted, but no one else. "I didn't want to be a distraction," he

CONTINUED ON PAGE 41

Mutual admiration

In a sea of hockey humanity and colorful confetti, captain Steve Yzerman and coach Scotty Bowman celebrated their third Stanley Cup in six years. Their relationship had come a long way since October 1996, when Bowman explored trading Yzerman to Ottawa. After Yzerman received the Cup from the commissioner, he immediately handed it to Bowman, who skated a final victory lap with the trophy held high.

MANDI WRIGHT/DETROIT FREE PRESS

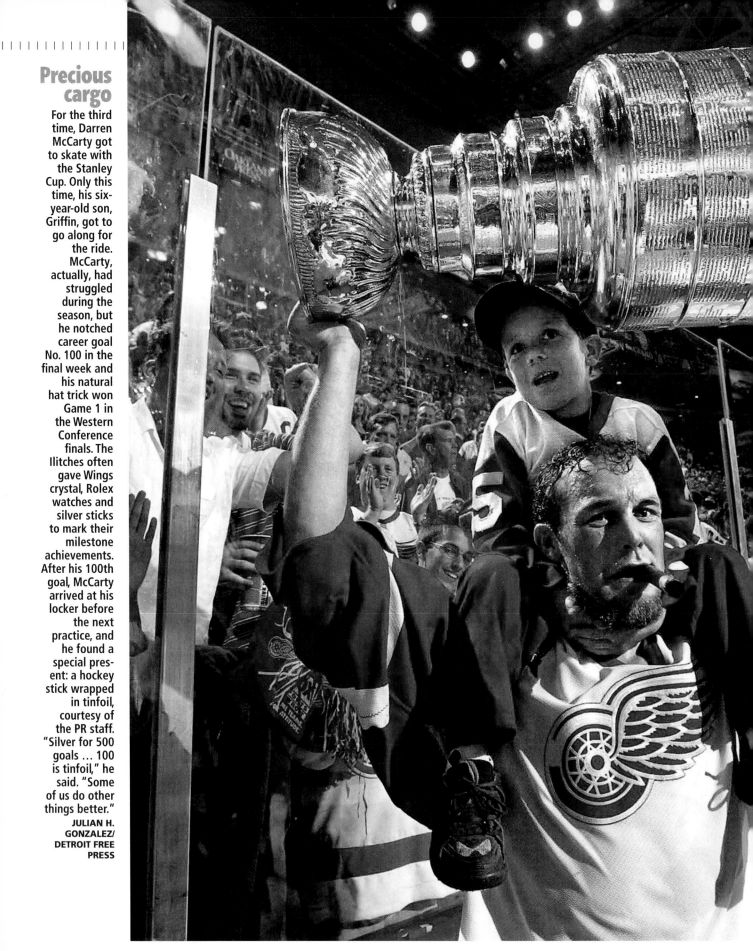

Precious cargo

For the third time, Darren McCarty got to skate with the Stanley Cup. Only this time, his six-year-old son, Griffin, got to go along for the ride. McCarty, actually, had struggled during the season, but he notched career goal No. 100 in the final week and his natural hat trick won Game 1 in the Western Conference finals. The Ilitches often gave Wings crystal, Rolex watches and silver sticks to mark their milestone achievements. After his 100th goal, McCarty arrived at his locker before the next practice, and he found a special present: a hockey stick wrapped in tinfoil, courtesy of the PR staff. "Silver for 500 goals … 100 is tinfoil," he said. "Some of us do other things better."

JULIAN H. GONZALEZ/ DETROIT FREE PRESS

Take your daughter to work day

Isabella Yzerman mimicked her famous father as The Captain held the Stanley Cup aloft for the faithful to see and to worship. After the 1997 championship, at 3:15 a.m., Steve Yzerman had squeezed the Cup into his Porche. Now a family man after the 2002 championship, at 2:15 a.m., he placed it in his Range Rover. With wife Lisa by his side and buddy Darren Pang in the back, Yzerman drove off.
KIRTHMON F. DOZIER/DETROIT FREE PRESS

CONTINUED FROM PAGE 38

said. As the players passed around the Cup, he let them know.

"It's bittersweet," Hull said. "To go out like this and to have the success he's had is so wonderful, but then to have it end is so sad. I feel as fortunate as anybody alive to say that he was my coach."

Forward Brendan Shanahan said: "I was shocked. He's been so involved and so excited throughout the whole playoffs that I just thought the way he was responding, this guy's going to go forever. But I guess it makes sense now. He knew it was his last playoff, and that's why he soaked it all up."

The Wings lost their first two playoffs games to Vancouver, but rallied to take the series in six. They eliminated St. Louis in five games. After falling behind, 3-2, they beat archrival Colorado in seven. After falling behind, 1-0, they beat Carolina in five.

No fewer than five Wings were legitimate candidates for the Conn Smythe Trophy as the playoffs' most valuable player: Hasek, Yzerman, Hull, Sergei Fedorov and Nicklas Lidstrom. In the end, Lidstrom won it. "It's a wonderful tribute to him," Bowman said. But everyone contributed, from the greats to the grinders. Take Game 5: Shanahan scored two goals, and Tomas Holmstrom, perhaps the grittiest grinder of them all, pitched in another.

"There's no better feeling," Hasek said.

With 9:19 left to play and the Wings up, 2-1, TV cameras caught white-gloved men taking the Cup out of its crate backstage. With 4:43 left, an octopus hit the ice ahead of Hasek. The Joe roared. And roared. And roared. "WE WANT THE CUP!" With 44.5 seconds left, the fans had it. From just across the red line, right in front of the Carolina bench, Shanahan fired a puck into an empty net. He leapt for joy. His teammates leapt with him. All season, they said they wouldn't celebrate until their job was done. Now it was.

"We were too old, too slow, too rich — fat cats," said Barry Smith, Bowman's longtime associate coach. "That's what we were told, and these guys were unbelievable. They sacrificed an awful lot, each one of these guys. They sacrificed ice time. They sacrificed personal power plays. They sacrificed a lot of things to make this a team. …

"They won the Presidents' Trophy as the best team all year, and they won the Stanley Cup. What else can you ask for? There's nothing else to win. They won it all."

Indeed, they were "Hockey Gods." So much so that became the title for a book about the season by Free Press beat writer Nicholas J. Cotsonika. He added this subtitle: "The Inside Story of the Red Wings' Hall of Fame Team."

TO THE ROOF

AT LAST, THE JOE GOT TO RAISE THE ULTIMATE BANNER

Cheers. And tears. The Captain. And Mr. Hockey. Lord Stanley's Cup. And a giant new red-and-white banner.

For the first time in 42 years, the Red Wings could hold a banner-raising ceremony as Stanley Cup champions. And the home opener turned out to be an emotional night to remember the past and present good times as well as those who could not be there.

Columnist Mitch Albom described it this way in the Free Press: "Applause filled the air. Up rose the red-and-white flag — 'Detroit Red Wings, 1996-97 Stanley Cup Champions' — past the lower level, past the first balcony. The crowd was on its feet, its noise at fever pitch. Music played. Swirling violins and royal trumpets. Lights flashed. Horns sounded.

"For a moment, they all watched the ascent of their accomplishment, the players tapping their sticks, the captain and his alternates, the old-timers. Finally, Steve Yzerman burst into a smile and gave an arm hug to white-haired Gordie Howe. 'Thanks for coming,' Yzerman whispered."

As the ceremony began, seven new banners hovered right above the ice. A mystery box labeled "Welcome to Hockeytown" sat at center ice.

Ted Lindsay, Gary Bergman and Howe, representing Red Wings past, were introduced and given a standing ovation. They watched the seven new banners — for the Cups in 1936, '37, '43, '50, '52, '54 and '55 — ascend to the rafters.

But this night was about the glory of 1997 and the teammates who remained in Beaumont Hospital in Royal Oak. Defenseman Vladimir Konstaninov, still unable to speak or walk, and masseur Sergei Mnatsakanov, paralyzed on his left side, were nearly killed in a limousine accident following a team party, six days after the Wings captured the Cup.

"We know Vladdie and Sergei are watching tonight," emcee Mickey Redmond said. "From all of us to all of you, come back soon. We love you. We believe."

The Wings unveiled commemorative patches — with "Believe" in English and Cyrillic — that the players would wear all season and that fans could purchase to assist the victims' families.

Attention returned to the Wings who were there. Each player was announced in numerical order, beginning with No. 2, Slava Fetisov, who had escaped

Comrades

During the banner-raising ceremony, Slava Fetisov and Igor Larionov comforted Yelena Mnatsakanov (left) and Irina Konstantinov, the wives of the Wings seriously injured in a June 1997 limousine accident. Defenseman Vladimir Konstantinov and masseur Sergei Mnatsakanov remained hospitalized but watched the ceremony on TV.
DAVID P. GILKEY/DETROIT FREE PRESS

the limo accident with minor injuries.

Notable by their absence were No. 29, Mike Vernon, the playoff MVP traded to San Jose, a victim of money and age, and No. 91, Sergei Fedorov, without a contract, stuck in negotiations.

Steve Yzerman, No. 19, arrived at the blue line and raised his stick high to salute the fans, as he did for Game 1 of the Stanley Cup finals. The fans roared and chanted "Ste-vie! Ste-vie! Ste-vie!"

Irina Konstantinov and Yelena Mnatsakanov, representing their hospitalized husbands, took the ice last. Tears rolled down Slava Kozlov's face. The players tapped their sticks on the ice. Igor Larionov and Fetisov skated over to give the wives a kiss.

"At first I didn't want to come," Yelena Mnatsakanov said. "I said, 'No, I can't do it, I can't do it, I won't be there.' Next I decided I must come because everybody is like family; we're very close. I just want to thank everybody for all the love."

That morning, trainer John Wharton took the Cup to Beaumont Hospital. Konstantinov and Mnatsakanov saw

where their names were engraved and drank juice from the trophy — although the masseur asked for vodka. "Vladdie didn't want to seem to let go," Wharton said. "It's the most encouraged I've been since the accident happened. The Stanley Cup has such a tremendous ability to lift people up."

Finally, the mystery box's contents were revealed: the Stanley Cup and the eighth Stanley Cup banner. The Captain and his

CONTINUED ON PAGE 43

CONTINUED FROM PAGE 42

alternates, Nicklas Lidstrom and Brendan Shanahan, picked up the Cup and skated it down the ice. "When you get a chance to lift the Stanley Cup in your own building," Yzerman said, "that's what you always dream of. It wasn't quite as exciting as when we won it, but I still get chills from it."

Howe, Lindsay, Bergman and retired Hall of Fame broadcaster Bruce Martyn each picked up a corner of the banner and carried along the red carpet. Later when asked whether he was bothered that there was a newer championship team than his in 1955, Howe laughed and said: "Nah. They still have three to go to catch us."

Then the banner that represented so much blood, sweat and tears headed for the rafters, stopping just below the seven other banners, apparently starting a new row, one that everyone hoped wouldn't take 42 years to start filling in.

Spoils of victory

Steve Yzerman and Brendan Shanahan skated with the Stanley Cup aloft while Red Wings old-timers carried the championship banner to be raised. Clockwise from top left: defenseman Gary Bergman, left wing Ted Lindsay, right wing Gordie Howe and radio broadcaster Bruce Martyn.
KIRTHMON F. DOZIER/DETROIT FREE PRESS

NO. 5: MAY 31, 2002

AN AVALANCHE OF GOALS IN GAME 7

WINGS RAIN GOALS ON COLORADO'S ROY, ISSUE HURRICANES WARNING

In Game 7 of the Western Conference finals, the Red Wings' first shot was a goal, by Tomas Holmstrom, and Patrick Roy shook his head. The Wings' second shot was a goal, by Sergei Fedorov, and Roy hung his head. The Wings' fifth shot was a goal, by Luc Robitaille, and Roy kicked the ice, flicked his neck, banged his stick, then skated away as if to leave.

Only one problem for the Colorado goalie and his soon-to-be-dethroned Avalanche teammates: There were still 2½ periods to go.

After the Wings' shocking 7-0 victory earned a berth in the Stanley Cup finals against the Carolina Hurricanes, columnist Mitch Albom wrote for the Free Press: "Now that's an avalanche. It rolled in off the Detroit River, it wore a red-and-white sweater, it skated as if its socks were on fire, and it scored one, two, three, four goals in the time it normally takes fans to find their seats. Then it scored five, six and seven. It didn't merely rise to the occasion, it pole-vaulted, getting relentless offense, smothering defense, shutout goaltending and more jump than a 1956 Elvis Presley concert. …

"The Detroit Red Wings just sent home the defending NHL champions in this city's most anticipated sporting event in a decade. And in doing so, they made one of the greatest goalies in hockey history look like just another man in a mask. Patrick Roy, on the bench, too whipped to even smirk correctly? Now that's an avalanche."

After Robitaille's goal at 10:25, the Avalanche called a time-out. Roy skated to the bench, took a drink and spoke to coach Bob Hartley. "He asked me, 'Do you want to come out?'" Roy said afterward. "I said, 'No. I'm staying in.'"

Not even 2½ minutes later, at 12:51, Holmstrom scored again, this time on a rebound. Roy, whose 240 playoff games were more than any goalie, allowed four goals in a playoff period for the first time.

"To be honest, we thought this would be an overtime game," captain Steve Yzerman said. "After the first period, we were up, 4-0, and we were still thinking, 'This isn't how it's supposed to be.'"

In the second period, Brett Hull notched the fifth goal at 4:41. The sixth goal, by Fredrik Olausson, sent Roy to the bench at 6:28. He smirked, then frowned. Television cameras caught Wings owners Mike and Marian Ilitch in their suite, Mike with his palms up, Marian with her arms up.

"You imagine and pray for something like this," Hull said, "but you don't realistically think

CONTINUED ON PAGE 45

‹‹ Three down, three to go

Patrick Roy, head down, spirits low, turned around and returned to the crease after Luc Robitaille scored the Wings' third goal, at 10:25 of the first period. At that point, Roy had allowed three goals and made two saves.
MANDI WRIGHT/DETROIT FREE PRESS

Pardon our French

Sometimes in the newspaper business everything just falls together perfectly. The Free Press Sports Department believed this front page marked one of those times. Designer Christoph Fuhrmans laid it out, design and graphics director Steve Dorsey wrote the headline and sports editor Gene Myers framed and hung this page in his office instead of the Stanley Cup page.

CONTINUED FROM PAGE 44

it's going to happen. A couple of us talked on the bench. We just said, 'We keep looking up at the clock in disbelief at the score.' "

Pavel Datsyuk scored the seventh goal, at 16:09 of the final period against David Aebischer.

Dominik Hasek became the first Wing since Tim Cheveldae in 1992 to post consecutive playoff shutouts and the first NHL player to record five shutouts in one playoff run. "It's nice," said Hasek, who never had won a Cup. "But I have different goal, and it's not about shutouts."

And here's how Albom concluded his column: "Savor this, Detroit, a night to remember. You just saw an Avalanche defeated by an avalanche. Now let's see how they handle Hurricanes."

TWO THE ROOF

SCOTTY, VLADDIE, SERGEI MAKE THE PARTY EXTRA SPECIAL

For the second straight October, the Red Wings raised a Stanley Cup banner and delivered plenty of pomp and circumstance at their Joe Louis Arena opener. The spotlight, though, shined the brightest on two men in wheelchairs and a coach in limbo who exited the locker room with his head covered as if chased by paparazzi.

Mayor Dennis Archer pronounced Detroit the top sports city in America. Commissioner Gary Bettman was booed until he began praising Steve Yzerman, Wings coaches, the Ilitch family and, finally, the fans. A tour of team lore followed: First Johnny Wilson, then Bill Gadsby, Carl Liscombe — at 83 one of the oldest living Wings — Gary Bergman and John Orgrodnick. Hall of Famers Ted Lindsay and Gordie Howe were the last to emerge. All stood when Howe strode to the ice, saluting him with the "Gordie! Gor-die!" chant. Finally, the Wings were introduced in numerical order, ending with No. 96, Tomas Holmstrom, who after 22 points in the regular season delivered seven goals and 12 assists in the 1998 playoffs.

Then it was time for Vladdie. "Bad to the Bone" blared from the speakers. The song had been an anthem at Wings games, played during a greatest-hits video on the scoreboard and dedicated to Vladimir Konstantinov, who nearly died in a limousine accident six days after the Wings won the 1997 Stanley Cup.

Radio broadcaster Ken Kal announced No. 16 and the building erupted. Konstantov was wheeled to the ice by trainer John Wharton and Sergei Fedorov, who missed the 1997 banner ceremony because of a contract dispute. Igor Larionov and Slava Kozlov — Slava Fetisov joined the Devils as an assistant coach — helped wheel out former team masseur Sergei Mnatsakanov, who also barely survived the limo accident.

There was one more guest: Scotty Bowman, looking slimmer and dapper. Recovering from off-season knee-replacement surgery and a heart procedure, Bowman, 65, had yet to announce whether he would return to coach the Wings. Even a man as stoic as Bowman — who had attended seven previous banner nights — couldn't quell his emotions when the fans rose and bestowed a reception that rivaled Steve Yzerman's. The players rapped their sticks on the ice.

Bowman smiled and quickly composed himself — until associate coach Dave Lewis grabbed Bowman's right arm and pumped it in the air, leaving Bowman beaming, laughing and mouthing a quick "thank you."

"When he came out on the bench," Doug Brown said with a laugh, "we figured he'd just stay right there."

As the banner ascended, Mnatsakanov, paralyzed on this left side, used his right hand to clap Kozlov's hand.

"Tonight was unbelievable," Kris Draper said. "Obviously, with Scotty coming back, Vladdie and Sergei out there where they belong, that was a lot more emotional than it was last year. It was great. The fans were right into it."

The wounded Russians watched the game from the Ilitches' skybox. Bowman, who did not talk to the media or the fans and offered no rally-the-troops speeches in the locker room, watched from the video room. After the Wings' 4-1 victory over St. Louis, Bowman came into the dressing room with his jacket pulled over his head and plowed through a media horde — and he left just as mysteriously, hightailing it out once he saw reporters flocked around Brendan Shanahan, who scored the game's last three goals.

Bowman returned to the bench after the associate coaches, Barry Smith and Lewis, started the season 4-1. The Wings won the Central Division with 93 points and swept the Anaheim Ducks in the first round. But Chris Osgood, who surrendered only six goals in the series, suffered a knee injury in his 31-save Game 4 shutout. Bill Ranford, a trade-deadline acquisition and the playoff MVP in 1990, started against the Avalanche and the Wings won Games 1 and 2 in Denver. Then everything collapsed: The Avs won four straight by outscoring the Wings, 19-7, and ambushing goalies Ranford, a gimpy Osgood and never-used Norm Maracle.

The Wings' next banner raising wouldn't come until October 2002. Bowman and his lieutenants directed the 1998 and 2002 champs. About a third of the 1998 players won again in 2002: Mathieu Dandenault, Nicklas Lidstrom, Kirk Maltby, Darren McCarty, Draper, Fedorov, Holmstrom, Larionov, Shanahan and Yzerman. These players also helped win the 1997 Cup.

They believed

The Wings wore "Believe" patches on their jerseys in 1997-98 to remind themselves that their goal wasn't just to repeat as Stanley Cup champions, but to do so for their fallen friends. When they raised the banner months after completing their mission, Vladimir Konstantinov and Sergei Mnatsakanov were on the ice in their wheelchairs. Owner Marian Ilitch greeted Konstantinov with a kiss.
JULIAN H. GONZALEZ/DETROIT FREE PRESS

MIDNIGHT SPECIAL

KOZLOV SENDS WINGS TO THEIR FIRST FINALS IN 29 YEARS

They said it in training camp in September. They said it when the lockout ended in January. They said it all season long.

The Cup. The Stanley Cup. That's what the Wings wanted. That was their goal.

And for the first time since 1966, the Wings advanced to the championship series when Slava Kozlov eliminated the Chicago Blackhawks, 2-1, with a goal 2:25 into the second overtime of Game 5. Scoreless in the first four games of the Western finals, Kozlov fired a low shot from the edge of the right circle that slipped between Ed Belfour's pads.

Bedlam ensued on the ice and in The Joe's stands. "Everybody just screamed," Kozlov said. "To the finals!" blared the morning's Free Press, a front page so popular it was sold on T-shirts.

Free Press columnist Mitch Albom wrote: "So this is how you make history. You wait until after the midnight hour, double overtime, when the voices are gone and even the sweat glands are exhausted, then send a young Russian — whose last name is easier to pronounced than his first — charging down the ice, have him wind up and fire and … bingo! With a game so exhausting it took two days to play, the Detroit Red Wings finally jumped the moat and are outside the castle, banging on the door with an octopus.

"Knock, knock, Stanley. Guess who's coming to dinner!"

"I dreamed about this all my life," forward Shawn Burr said. "I can't believe it. My heart just stopped."

"It's unbelievable," goalie Mike Vernon said.

Belfour, a Vezina Trophy runner-up to Buffalo's Dominik Hasek, did everything but stand on his head the entire series. And in Game 5 he singlehandedly delayed the Wings' celebration. The Wings outshot the Hawks, 38-14, through regulation, including 20-2 in the middle period. Their lone goal came from an ailing Steve Yzerman, who used Bob Errey as a screen and found an open spot over Belfour's shoulder. Yzerman had missed Games 1-3 because of arthroscopic knee surgery and retreated to the locker room briefly for treatment during Game 5's first period.

Although they went out in five games, the Blackhawks provided the Wings' toughest competition of the abbreviated season. In 48 games, the Wings captured the Presidents' Trophy, won 33 games and surrendered the second-fewest goals (two more than Chicago). In the playoffs, they ousted the Dallas Stars in five and swept the San Jose Sharks.

All four victories over the Blackhawks were by a single goal. One came in overtime (Nicklas Lidstrom at 1:01 in Game 1). One came in the final moments (Kris Draper at 18:15 in Game 2). Two came in double overtime (Vladimir Konstantinov at 9:25 in Game 3 and Kolzov at 2:25 in Game 5). For the series, actually, the Hawks outscored the Wings, 12-11.

Still, the Wings were 12-2 in the playoffs with home-ice advantage against the New Jersey Devils for their first Stanley Cup finals since 1966's six-game loss to Montreal. The underdog Devils, though, had two advantages: a hot young goalie in Martin Broduer and the left wing lock, a perplexing defensive system that the Wings hadn't faced because in the shortened season Western and Eastern teams never faced off.

The Wings could do little against the Devils' defenses. They lost Game 1, 2-1, and Game 2, 4-2. It only got worse at the Meadowlands: The Devils completed their sweep with a pair of 5-2 victories. The Wings had been outscored, 16-7. With three goals and two assists, Sergei Fedorov contributed to five of the goals. Steve Yzerman scored only once and finished with a minus-7 rating. Lidstrom also finished minus-7. Vernon went 0-4 with a 4.08 goals-against average. Burr was benched for Games 3 and 4.

"Right now," Yzerman said, "I don't feel much like a Stanley Cup finalist."

"In American sports," defenseman Paul Coffey said, "one day you're on top, the next day, you're a piece of (bleep)." He coughed. "Pardon my French."

For the sixth time since their last Stanley Cup in 1955, the Wings failed in the championship series — and the team and its fans felt like you know what, in French and English.

To the finals!

The Red Wings celebrated like it was 1966 — or something like that — after Slava Kozlov's goal in double overtime eliminated the Blackhawks and shoved Detroit into the Stanley Cup finals for the first time in a generation. The Wings hadn't won the actual Cup since 1955.
JULIAN H. GONZALEZ/DETROIT FREE PRESS

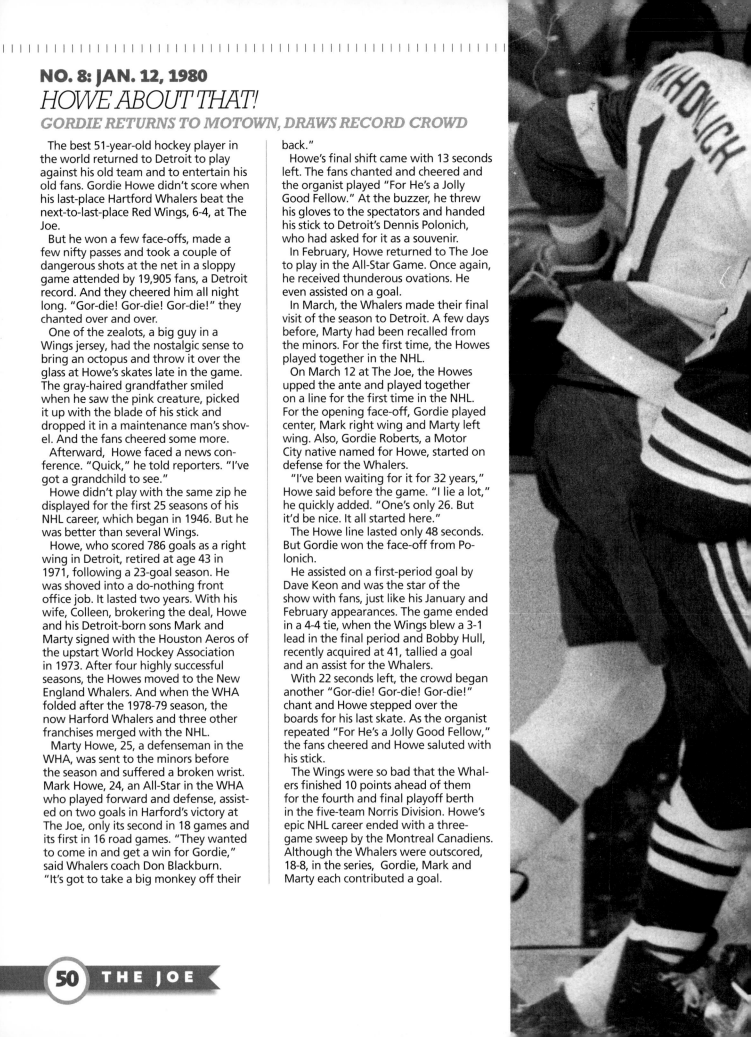

HOWE ABOUT THAT!

GORDIE RETURNS TO MOTOWN, DRAWS RECORD CROWD

The best 51-year-old hockey player in the world returned to Detroit to play against his old team and to entertain his old fans. Gordie Howe didn't score when his last-place Hartford Whalers beat the next-to-last-place Red Wings, 6-4, at The Joe.

But he won a few face-offs, made a few nifty passes and took a couple of dangerous shots at the net in a sloppy game attended by 19,905 fans, a Detroit record. And they cheered him all night long. "Gor-die! Gor-die! Gor-die!" they chanted over and over.

One of the zealots, a big guy in a Wings jersey, had the nostalgic sense to bring an octopus and throw it over the glass at Howe's skates late in the game. The gray-haired grandfather smiled when he saw the pink creature, picked it up with the blade of his stick and dropped it in a maintenance man's shovel. And the fans cheered some more.

Afterward, Howe faced a news conference. "Quick," he told reporters. "I've got a grandchild to see."

Howe didn't play with the same zip he displayed for the first 25 seasons of his NHL career, which began in 1946. But he was better than several Wings.

Howe, who scored 786 goals as a right wing in Detroit, retired at age 43 in 1971, following a 23-goal season. He was shoved into a do-nothing front office job. It lasted two years. With his wife, Colleen, brokering the deal, Howe and his Detroit-born sons Mark and Marty signed with the Houston Aeros of the upstart World Hockey Association in 1973. After four highly successful seasons, the Howes moved to the New England Whalers. And when the WHA folded after the 1978-79 season, the now Harford Whalers and three other franchises merged with the NHL.

Marty Howe, 25, a defenseman in the WHA, was sent to the minors before the season and suffered a broken wrist. Mark Howe, 24, an All-Star in the WHA who played forward and defense, assisted on two goals in Harford's victory at The Joe, only its second in 18 games and its first in 16 road games. "They wanted to come in and get a win for Gordie," said Whalers coach Don Blackburn. "It's got to take a big monkey off their back."

Howe's final shift came with 13 seconds left. The fans chanted and cheered and the organist played "For He's a Jolly Good Fellow." At the buzzer, he threw his gloves to the spectators and handed his stick to Detroit's Dennis Polonich, who had asked for it as a souvenir.

In February, Howe returned to The Joe to play in the All-Star Game. Once again, he received thunderous ovations. He even assisted on a goal.

In March, the Whalers made their final visit of the season to Detroit. A few days before, Marty had been recalled from the minors. For the first time, the Howes played together in the NHL.

On March 12 at The Joe, the Howes upped the ante and played together on a line for the first time in the NHL. For the opening face-off, Gordie played center, Mark right wing and Marty left wing. Also, Gordie Roberts, a Motor City native named for Howe, started on defense for the Whalers.

"I've been waiting for it for 32 years," Howe said before the game. "I lie a lot," he quickly added. "One's only 26. But it'd be nice. It all started here."

The Howe line lasted only 48 seconds. But Gordie won the face-off from Polonich.

He assisted on a first-period goal by Dave Keon and was the star of the show with fans, just like his January and February appearances. The game ended in a 4-4 tie, when the Wings blew a 3-1 lead in the final period and Bobby Hull, recently acquired at 41, tallied a goal and an assist for the Whalers.

With 22 seconds left, the crowd began another "Gor-die! Gor-die! Gor-die!" chant and Howe stepped over the boards for his last skate. As the organist repeated "For He's a Jolly Good Fellow," the fans cheered and Howe saluted with his stick.

The Wings were so bad that the Whalers finished 10 points ahead of them for the fourth and final playoff berth in the five-team Norris Division. Howe's epic NHL career ended with a three-game sweep by the Montreal Canadiens. Although the Whalers were outscored, 18-8, in the series, Gordie, Mark and Marty each contributed a goal.

Gordie and Mark Howe of the Whalers battled with a pair of Red Wings in brand-new Joe Louis Arena in January 1980. Mark had two assists and Gordie missed three shots in a 6-4 Hartford victory. Gordie had spent 25 seasons with the Wings before retiring in 1971. Mark had played for the Junior Wings during his formative years. Gordie was inducted into the Hockey Hall of Fame in 1972. When Mark joined him in 2011, they were the fourth father-son tandem to be inducted. In his book, "Gordie Howe's Son," Mark wrote: "I first realized I had a famous father when he would take me places and everybody wanted his autograph. But I just thought that was normal. For as long as I remembered, Gordie Howe had been my dad more than Mr. Hockey."

ALAN R. KAMUDA/ DETROIT FREE PRESS

LATE NIGHT WITH THE CAPTAIN

YZERMAN'S MOST MEMORABLE GOAL? 'THE SHOT HEARD 'ROUND THE JOE' AFTER HIS VOW NOT TO LOSE GAME 7

It was every suspense film you ever watched, every thriller you ever read, every nervous waiting room you ever sat in, all the nail-biting, chest-heaving experiences you ever endured, rolled into one cold, double-overtime evening at Joe Louis Arena, 19,983 exhausted fans and a few million more scattered around their television sets, tapping their chests at every break to make sure the old ticker was still working.

And finally, the doctor emerged, smiling with the good news: It's a goal!

"YES! YES! YES!" the fans screamed, when Steve Yzerman put an end to the most dramatic playoff game here in years, whacking a 55-foot shot past the seemingly impenetrable Jon Casey to win Game 7 of this second-round series, 1-0. The crowd erupted like a volcano, and Yzerman himself was lifted into the air by the force of his own elation, running and cheering without ever touching the ice.

It's a goal. Breathe again.

As Free Press columnist Mitch Albom wrote, Red Wings fans could indeed breathe again. Another great team in the winter appeared poised for a heart-breaking spring. These 1996 Wings had won 62 games, an NHL record, yet in the Western semifinals they fell behind the sub-.500 Blues, three games to two.

Then Steve Yzerman spoke for his teammates and said the Wings would win Game 6 and bring the series back to The Joe. And before Game 7 he declared: "We're going to win."

"As far as a captain, he's a total captain," owner Mike Ilitch said after what most hockey fans consider the most memorable goal of Yzerman's career. "He does it all. You take your Mark Messier. We've got our Steve Yzerman.

"In 14 years he has never been a chatterbox. But in Game 6 and 7 he was talking on the bench. It had an effect on the guys."

After four periods, Yzerman had taken seven shots. His line with Sergei Fedorov and Darren McCarty or Doug Brown had shut down the Blues' top line of Wayne Gretzky, Brett Hull and Shayne Corson. Moments into the second overtime, Yzerman beat two defenders and threaded a pass to Fedorov at top of the crease. Despite a Blue yanking his right shoulder, Fedorov managed a shot but Jon Casey made a sprawling save.

Yzerman started his second shift as Wings' defense was clearing the zone without a Blue in sight. Slava Fetisov passed to Vladimir Konstantinov, who wanted to hit Bob Errey streaking through the left side of the neutral zone. Konstantinov slightly mishit the pass and Gretzky appeared out of nowhere, reached behind his back with one hand on his stick and deflected the pass at the blue line. The puck hit his skate as he tried to corral it, and turned again searching for it.

Yzerman swooped in from behind and collected the loose puck. In an instant he crossed the red line. As he neared the blue line at full speed, Dino Cicceralli moved out of his way, two Blues defensemen started retreating and a hustling Gretzky angled his way within 10 feet. Yzerman began his windup right before the blue line and unleashed a slap shot right after he crossed it.

Somehow, someway, his 55-footer flew past Casey, hit the crossbar, bounced into the net and finally chased away the Blues 75 seconds into the second overtime and 18 minutes before midnight.

"I just picked up a turnover in the neutral zone," Yzerman said, quietly, sitting on a stool in front of his locker. "I was just trying to go between the defenseman's legs. …

"I don't score a whole lot from the blue line, so I definitely was surprised. I shot it and looked up and heard the clang against the bar and I was like, 'No way. It went in.'"

Coach Scott Bowman dissected the play this way: "It happened so fast I don't think anybody expected it. We were having trouble getting a shot at the net. It was a great shot."

"It's the kind of goal," Yzerman said, "every player dreams about in his career."

One for the ages

Captain Steve Yzerman acknowledged the epic ovation from the fans after his double-overtime goal eliminated the St. Louis Blues in Game 7. After a season with 62 victories, the Wings had reached the conference finals.
DETROIT FREE PRESS

GOOD-BYE, GORDIE

FROM 9 A.M. PAST 9 P.M., 15,000 FANS PAY THEIR RESPECTS AT MR. HOCKEY'S VISITATION

The old. The young. The known. The anonymous. They lined up outside around the southwest corner of Joe Louis Arena, sometimes more than 300 deep in the early afternoon. The woolen, long-sleeved No. 9 winged wheel sweaters that many wore not exactly meshing well with the springtime heat. But those paying tribute to Gordie Howe patiently waited for as long as two hours without complaint.

With those words and many others, Free Press columnist Drew Sharp captured the scenes and emotions of an epic day in which Wings Nation said good-bye to Mr. Hockey. For more than 12 hours — 9 a.m. past 9 p.m. — an estimated 15,000 fans came to The Joe to pay their respects to Mr. Hockey four days after his death at 88. In the spirit of the ever-humble icon, his extensive family stayed for the entire visitation and took turns shaking hands and chatting with the never-ending line of mourners.

Outside The Joe, two huge "Thank you, Mr. Hockey" placards hung on an arena wall. They quickly were filled with observations from the grieving as well as the gracious. A father took his little boy by the hand near the tribute. The little boy pointed to all the messages and said to his father: "He knew a lot of people."

Inside The Joe, Howe lay in repose on a raised, red-carpeted stage, a closed casket adorned with red and white flowers. The Stanley Cup banners from the 1950s were lowered, a pair on each side of the No. 9 banner. On one side of the stage was seating for Howe's family. On the other side was a display of trophies and jerseys, including three from the Houston Aeros, for Howe and his sons Mark and Marty. A giant "9" was projected in white on the darken flooring that covered what usually would be ice.

Around 12:30 p.m., Wings GM Ken Holland took a peek from behind a curtain, the bier with Mr. Hockey's remains only a few feet away, and marveled how the procession of mourners never dissipated.

"How many of those people never saw Gordie play one time?" he said. "Not one time because they're not old enough. But there was a strong connection because they know that he was not only a great ambassador for the Detroit Red Wings, but for the sport of hockey overall."

Former coach Scotty Bowman said:

"It's an amazing tribute, because Gordie could relate to anybody and everybody. Here you have perhaps the greatest hockey player of all time and he was accessible to people from all walks of life. If you met him, you never forgot it. Even if it was a long time ago."

Howe played one of the world's most demanding sports until he was 52 years old, and many fans argue that no one played it better. His pro career of 2,421 games ran from World War II through Vietnam, Truman to Carter, Sinatra to the Sex Pistols. He lasted so long that he played professionally with his children.

Howe combined skill, savvy, strength, meanness and longevity like no other player. He was among the greatest sports stars of the 20th Century, and he had reigned in the trinity of Detroit's top athletes, with Joe Louis and Ty Cobb.

Howe died on June 10, 2016, in Sylvania, Ohio. He had been staying there with his son the doctor, Murray. Howe had suffered from dementia in his later years and suffered a stroke in October 2014. Stem-cell treatment helped him rally from near-death, and celebrations for his last birthday, March 31, included a visit to The Joe.

Howe spent 25 years as a Red Wing and lived in southeast Michigan for most of his long retirement. He was an

CONTINUED ON PAGE 55

CONTINUED FROM PAGE 54

extraordinarily public person who encountered thousands of people over the decades. He remained a megastar who happened to be unassuming, playful and patient, and he often had a kind word or gentle gibe for every fan. Howe frequently used his dry wit to disarm awestruck audiences. Speaking to French Canadians, he would say, "I'm bilingual: English and profanity."

Howe starred at right wing for the Wings from 1946 to 1971. In that quarter-century, they won nine regular-season league titles and four Stanley Cup championships. He led the league in scoring six times, was selected MVP

Gordietown

The lunchtime crowd for Gordie Howe's visitation stretched around The Joe. The Red Wings estimated that more than 15,000 fans paid their final respects.
ERIC SEALS/DETROIT FREE PRESS

six times and made the All-Star Game 23 times. He finished in the top five in scoring for 20 straight seasons.

Howe retired after the 1970-71 season and became a club vice president. The Wings retired his jersey in March 1972 during an elaborate ceremony at Olympia that included Vice President Spiro Agnew. But Howe chafed at the do-nothing role the Wings assigned him, reportedly calling it the "mushroom treatment" in which they keep you in the dark and occasionally throw manure on you. When Howe told the story, he used an earthier word than manure, and always got a laugh.

In 1973, Howe became a pro player again. The Houston Aeros of the upstart World Hockey Association offered him a chance to play with Marty and Mark, and the Howes became stars and hockey promoters in the Sun Belt, then all three moved to the New England Whalers in 1977. When four WHA teams merged with the NHL in 1979, Howe — at 51 — started one final season.

He played in all 80 games, scoring 15 goals. Scotty Bowman selected him to play in the 1980 All-Star Game at the new Joe Louis Arena, and Howe seemed to tear up when a crowd of 21,002 gave him a 2½-minute standing ovation and chanted his name.

Five days after Howe's death, hockey royalty and average fans, many in No. 9 jerseys with the winged wheel, packed the Cathedral of the Most Blessed Sacrament in Detroit for the funeral. Murray Howe delivered the televised eulogy, using anecdote after anecdote for nearly a half-hour to demonstrate how his father, who grew up poor in Saskatoon, Saskatchewan, lived an outsized life.

"I asked my dad a few years ago what he would like me to say at his funeral," Murray said. "He said, 'Say this: Finally, the end of the third period.' Then he added, 'I hope there is a good hockey team in heaven.'

"Dad, all I can say is, once you join the team, they won't just be good, they will be great."

RETURN TO THE FINAL FOUR

HOCKEY FEVER SWEEPS DETROIT AS WINGS COMPLETE COMEBACK

The fans were going insane, the players were slapping each other in celebration and even coach Jacques Demers, dressed in his lucky wedding suit, walked out across the ice, raised a fist, and suddenly leaped toward the heavens. Why not? That's where these magic words seemed to be coming from: The Red Wings are going to the semifinals.

When Free Press columnist Mitch Albom described the scene after Game 7 of the Norris Division finals — a 3-0 wipeout of Toronto — the Red Wings had been one of the NHL's underprivileged for two decades. Now their first-year coach and their 21-year-old captain were talking crazy talk:

"The miracle that wasn't supposed to happen, happened," Jacques Demers gushed. "It's a great day for Detroit hockey fans."

"I've never won a Stanley Cup, but if the feeling is any better than this, I can't wait!" Steve Yzerman declared. "It feels good to be a Detroit Red Wing right now."

Sure, they had lost the regular-season Norris title to St. Louis on the season's final day. Sure, they had finished two games under .500. Sure, they had just eliminated a team 10 games under .500.

But the Wings hadn't been one of the final four teams since the Original Six doubled in size in 1967. But the Wings were coming off the worst season in their history — club records for fewest victories (17), most losses (57), fewest points (40) and most goals allowed (415). But the Wings had to rally from a three-games-to-one hole against the Maple Leafs, only the fourth team to survive such a deficit.

Detroit was so captivated by the Wings' playoff run that minutes before Game 7 hundreds of fans were begging for tickets outside The Joe. Scalpers got up to $100 for mediocre seats and $40 to $50 for standing room. Halfway through the first period about 20 police officers shooed off unsuccessful ticket buyers.

Midway through the final period, fans taunted Leafs coach John Brophy, who carried on a season-long feud with Demers, with a haunting chant of "Brophy!

CONTINUED ON PAGE 56

CONTINUED FROM PAGE 55

Brophy!" Then someone threw a broom in front of the Toronto bench — a reminder to all the Leafs fans who talked about a sweep after the Wings lost the first two games at home.

Superb all series in relief of Greg Stefan, goalie Glen Hanlon saved his best for Game 7. He stopped 30 shots for his second straight shutout at The Joe. Adam Oates, Darren Veitch and Yzerman, previously goalless in the series, supplied the goals.

In their dressing room, the Wings drank champagne and poured it over each other's heads. It was a christening of sorts; they never had done that since moving from Olympia, where champagne flowed freely a long time ago.

Two nights later, the Wings stunned the Edmonton Oilers of Wayne Gretzy, Jari Kurri and Mark Messier — all 100-point scorers — with a 3-1 victory. At the time, the Wings had lost 10 straight to the Oilers and 18 out of 20. However, the Oilers won the next four games, a couple of which were tight, and then beat Philadelphia for the Stanley Cup, the third of Gretzky's career.

NO. 12: OCT, 13, 1995
VOX POPULI: GO STEVIE Y
CHEERS FOR THE CAPTAIN, BOOS FOR THE COACH

Opening night at The Joe turned out to be a perfect evening for Red Wings fans. They watched as the Wings raised four banners representing the 1995 season's success. They cheered, long and loud, as captain Steve Yzerman was introduced. They booed, long and loud, when coach and director of player personnel Scotty Bowman's name was announced, sending a clear message not to trade Yzerman.

And then Yzerman and his teammates gave fans a show they hadn't seen in sometime: a 9-0 destruction of the Oilers. Yzerman contributed an assist and the final goal.

Clearly, Yzerman was moved by the fans' reaction. He skated in a little circle when he was introduced, then shyly looked down at the ice. The decibels of the roar heightened as it continued well into a second minute, when as an encore Yzerman stepped forward for another pirouette, raising his stick in a salute to the crowd.

Bowman was the last to be introduced, and the fans were waiting for him, too. They lustily booed because he had been negotiating a trade of Yzerman to his hometown Ottawa Senators for Alexei Yashin. The booing seemed to amuse Bowman. He faked as if he were stalking off the bench, then came back smiling.

"That's OK," he said later. "I'd rather have the focus on me than on the players." However, he earlier had described as "personal attacks" the media's criticism for his attempts to trade The Captain.

Keith Gave wrote in the Free Press: "If the court of public opinion matters — and Red Wings fans shouldn't kid themselves, it does — then Steve Yzerman deserves to wear the winged wheel for life. And coach Scotty Bowman, tried and convicted by a jury of 20,000 peers in pregame ceremonies, was sentenced to a career of abuse as long as he remains behind the Detroit bench — pardonable only if he delivers a Stanley Cup."

Charlie Vincent wrote: "Scotty Bowman never seems to try to win popularity contests. His personality has the warmth of a snowball. I don't think I'd want to work for the man. But you've got to admit he has a way of making winners out of teams. Perhaps his methods are abrasive and sometimes maybe they are even dehumanizing. But they have worked enough to make him the winningest coach in the history of the game."

Yzerman, of course, wasn't traded. The Wings would win 62 games, an NHL record, in 1995-96 and their first Stanley Cup in 42 years in 1996-97. Plus, Yzerman would come to be regarded as possibly the best captain in NHL history.

That night of his big ovation, he needed help from his teammates when the rope he yanked wouldn't reveal the four banners to be hoisted to the rafters.

"You're only excited," Yzerman said, "if you're raising the Stanley Cup banner."

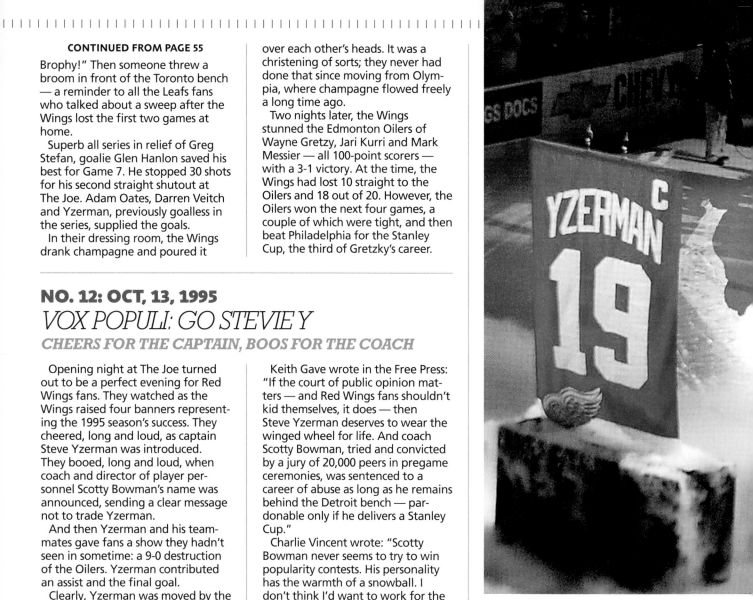

NO. 13: JAN. 2, 2007
FOREVER 19
THE CAPTAIN TAKES HIS PLACE AMONG THE GREATEST WINGS

Steve Yzerman was known as a man of few words when he played, but when he did speak people usually listened.

The sold-out crowd at The Joe for his jersey retirement vehemently disagreed when he tried to share credit with former teammates and coaches by saying: "I feel my image as a great leader was greatly overblown …"

"NO!" the crowd yelled.

Earlier in the 90-minute ceremony, owner Mike Ilitch said: "For Steve Yzerman, being team captain it wasn't just his responsibility. It ran through his veins." Former coach Scotty Bowman said: "Steve built a legacy for all future Red Wing personnel to uphold. You were everything a captain should be."

CONTINUED ON PAGE 57

Note the 'C'

The Joe stood at attention moments before Steve Yzerman's jersey ascended to the rafters. His No. 19 banner included a special touch — the "C" in the right corner to honor his 1986-2006 captaincy. Yzerman discussed leadership and coach Scotty Bowman: "One thing I learned about him was how to become tougher mentally. Playing under him, my confidence grew. Well, my stats declined, but my confidence grew. … He changed me as a hockey player in a lot of ways and made me a much better leader and a much better captain."

DIANE WEISS/ DETROIT FREE PRESS

CONTINUED FROM PAGE 56

More highlights from the night No. 19 went to the rafters as the Wings' sixth retired jersey:

▶ Most over the top moment: When they played "Also Sprach Zarathustra" — the theme from "2001: A Space Odyssey" — while re-raising the jerseys of Gordie Howe, Ted Lindsay, Sid Abel, Alex Delvecchio and Terry Sawchuk.

▶ Better choice: Yzerman walked out to "Simply the Best," by Tina Turner.

▶ There were a lot of big cheers, but besides the man of the hour-and-half, the biggest decibels went to Howe and Co., Bob Probert (who took a seat next to Joe Kocur), Brett Hull, Igor Larionov and Bowman, with players wearing white Wings jerseys with No. 19 patches.

▶ Most touching moment: When Vladimir Konstantinov used a walker to come out to the C-shaped red carpet on the ice.

▶ Even the Stanley Cup made an appearance.

▶ All of the Wings wore Yzerman jerseys for their warm-up — that's standard for nights like these — but they weren't just Detroit jerseys. Some wore Team Canada jerseys, some wore Campbell Conference All-Star jerseys, and some even wore Peterborough Petes sweaters from his way-back-when OHL team.

▶ Congrats messages were displayed on the big screen from Darren McCarty, Joe Sakic, Jarome Iginla and Wayne Gretzky, among others. Fans at The Joe booed just one, the one from Bill Ford Jr.

▶ Jacques Demers made a rare appearance at The Joe. In 1986, he famously made a 21-year-old Yzerman the youngest captain in franchise history.

▶ Nice parting gift from the Ilitches: A Chevy Tahoe. "Boy, will that look nice going over to Oakland Hills, Steve," said emcee Darren Pang, Yzerman's buddy.

▶ Nice parting gift from the players: A family trip to the 2008 European soccer championships in Austria.

▶ More from Ilitch: "Steve Yzerman, you helped build Hockeytown."

▶ More from Bowman: "Steve, in trying to figure a reason for your longevity of the Red Wings, I've come to the conclusion that maybe we've kept you feeling so young by bringing in so many players older than you."

Eventually, it was Yzerman's turn to speak. "Thank you," he began, stopping as fans yelled his name, clapped, yelled some more, whistled. A minute went by, then another. Yzerman turned, waved, clutched his hands. The "Ste-vie! Ste-vie!" chants ebbed, then rose again.

"You never disappoint me," he said.

Just before No. 19 went up, Yzerman told the fans: "You look up there, give yourself a pat on the back because I really feel you're a huge reason, a big reason, why it's up there. From the bottom of my heart, I am sincerely grateful to you all."

BROTHERLY LOVE

PROBERT AND KOCUR: BRUISE BROTHERS SUDDENLY TURN INTO BLOODIED BROTHERS

Boys will be boys. Bruisers will be bruisers.

Detroit's Bob Probert and New York's Joe Kocur, tough guy teammates for six seasons with the Red Wings, accidentally squared off in the first period of a Wings-Rangers game at The Joe. Their bout sent the 19,875 fans into a frenzy.

Kocur, traded to Rangers in 1991, and Probert were legendary in the league for mixing it up. But who would have figured the close friends, who took lessons at Kronk to hone their pugilistic skills, ever would fight each other?

"Before, we only fought over who should clean the house," Kocur said. "It came in the heat of the battle, and we'll laugh the next time we talk. I think the fans always wanted to see it.

"He swung at someone on our team, and I went over to stop him. The next thing I know, he hit me a couple times in the chops. It was fun."

The two were caught up in a scuffle involving several players. "I didn't know it was Joey until I was already in it," Probert said. "At that point, you can't stop."

Kocur bloodied Probert's nose, but Probert came on strong with a series of vicious upper cuts. Kocur's jersey and helmet were pulled off as Probert slammed him into the boards. The pair locked up until Probert broke free, shed his helmet and tried to remove his jersey to mount another assault. That's when the linesmen broke it up.

"That's hockey," said Wings GM Bryan Murray. "Even the best of friends will go at it. These are tough kids. But they will still be friends."

In June, Kocur was hoisting the Stanley Cup with the Rangers. In July, the Free Press ran the big headline "Party's over," when the Wings finally cut ties with Probert, fed up with his endless issues with cocaine, alcohol, suspensions, jail time and immigration restrictions.

By December 1996, Probert had settled in nicely with Chicago and Kocur was playing in a beer league. That same month Probert had run Wings goalie Chris Osgood. In search of some muscle, the Wings signed Kocur to see whether he had any gas left in his 32-year-old tank and rocket fuel in his mangled right hand. On Jan. 5 in Chicago, he answered the bell by fighting Probert to a draw and pounding Cam Russell's face to a bloody pulp in front of the Blackhawks' bench.

For two straight springs, Kocur dropped in on the Grind Line from time to time and hoisted the Cup with the Wings. After he retired, the Wings hired him for several roles.

Probert's career ended around the same time. His life still appeared to be a mess, but eventually his name stopped appearing as frequently in the police blotters. He no longer was persona non grata with the Wings. He attended Steve Yzerman's jersey retirement ceremony. He scored a goal in the Showdown in Hockeytown alumni game against Boston. Each time, he received warm welcomes.

"I don't have to worry about fighting unless Joey comes after me," Probert said at the showdown. Kocur was his coach for the game at The Joe.

Probert, though, died of a heart attack on July 5, 2010, while boating on Lake St. Clair with his family. He was 45.

Yzerman spoke at his funeral across the Detroit River in Windsor: "Most will remember Bob for his fighting ability and his scoring touch. He was much more than that."

Dukes of hazard

Despite a huge disadvantage in height, weight and pugilistic experience, Red Wings goalie Chris Osgood battled toe-to-toe with Colorado's Patrick Roy. Eventually, Osgood wrestled Roy to the ice. "Not too bad for somebody who's never fought before," teammate Darren McCarty said.

JULIAN H. GONZALEZ/
DETROIT FREE PRESS

NO. 15: APRIL 1, 1998
MOTHERLY LOVE
ONCE AGAIN THE GOALIES FIGHT AND ONCE AGAIN A RED WING MAKES SURE THAT ROY GOES DOWN

Almost one year to the day after Darren McCarty bloodied Claude Lemieux and Mike Vernon bloodied Patrick Roy, hockey's most intense rivalry returned to a super-charged atmosphere at The Joe.

Would McCarty and Lemieux tussle for a third time in 12 months? Would Roy call out Chris Osgood, Vernon's successor in net?

Exactly what mayhem and drama would unfold?

As the game neared the 50-minute mark, the answer appeared to be none. "You came away with the feeling that the Wings and Avalanche had kissed, made up and buried the hatchets," Drew Sharp would write in the Free Press.

Then Sergei Fedorov broke a scoreless game with two goals in four minutes. A short time later, a routine scuffle near the Colorado bench turned into another five-on-five battle royal. And Roy intended to make it six-on-six, skating to center ice and beckoning Osgood to join him.

One fan in the now-frenzied crowd — a smartly dressed woman all the way from British Columbia — didn't want to Osgood fight Roy. That woman was Osgood's mother, Joy.

Using her son's season tickets in Section 203B, Osgood couldn't believe her eyes as the pugilistic action started to unfold on the final night of a weeklong visit. By chance, her seats were next to the Free Press' sports editor, Gene Myers.

"Chris, get back in the goal. Chris, get back in the goal," she shouted at the top of her lungs. "No. No. No. Chris, get back in the goal."

When the punches started, she couldn't watch. Then she stole a glance, then another. And then she started yelling at her son again. "Get him, Chris. Get him. Get him."

When Osgood, despite a two-inch and 15-pound disadvantage, wrestled Roy to the ice near the Wings' bench, his mother started a new yell: "Oz-zie! Oz-zie! Oz-zie!"

At that point, she sounded like every other fan who despised the Avs.

She was downright giddy and overwhelmed with pride when her son left the rink to a standing ovation with 17 minutes in penalties.

Sharp wrote: "Osgood, recently questioned by fans and media, was unquestionably the victor in the physical and psychological sense. By not backing down, Osgood may have forever silenced any reservations about his competitiveness and his toughness. Just as Mike Vernon did last year. …

"The little guy swallowed his fears, stood up to the big man and brought him down — and looked even bigger in everyone's eyes than anybody would have imagined."

Kris Draper and McCarty, Osgood's good friends, praised him for standing up to Roy, who later told reporters "we had to do something; it was a negative on us last year."

Draper: "(Roy) underestimated Ozzie. He didn't think Ozzie was going to come out, but he wasn't running away. It was good to see."

McCarty: "I don't think Ozzie wanted to do it, but he saw there was no choice. … It was fun to watch Ozzie go at it. Not too bad for somebody who's never fought before. He held his own pretty well.

"You're not going to see that too often. And I personally hope I don't have to see that again."

Osgood and Roy, of course, were ejected. Every player on the ice received at least a misconduct penalty at 12:49. For the Red Wings, that was Slava Kozlov, Martin Lapointe, Kirk Maltby, Mike Rouse and Aaron Ward.

Notable by their absence were McCarty and Lemieux, who only could watch the melee from their respective benches.

"I'm in the middle of that stuff all the time," McCarty said. "I guess other guys wanted to do it this time. I had a good seat for it, anyway."

THE HOCKEY GODS REUNITE

AN UNUSUAL NIGHT TO REMEMBER FOR HASEK, BOWMAN AND YZERMAN

Like a tourist revisiting a beloved place, newly retired Dominik Hasek basked in his return to The Joe. Before he wandered onto the red carpet, left hand in pocket and right hand acknowledging a warm welcome from the fans, he took with him one last memory, one more attempt to never forget his season in Detroit.

"I was emotional and I touched the ice one more time because I don't know when I'll be back," Hasek said after the Red Wings' banner-raising ceremony to commemorate the 2002 Stanley Cup championship.

Like Hasek, Steve Yzerman and Scotty Bowman found themselves in unique situations during the festivities. Like Hasek, Bowman retired after the season. When he stepped on the red carpet, the Hall of Fame coach received a deafening ovation. "These things get more glamorous every time," he said. "This one was great."

The players were introduced in numerical order, skated to their blue line and fell into formation — with one exception. Before radio announcer Ken Kal could call out No. 19's name, the cheers spiked straight to the roof. Yzerman came out in a black suit and tie, turned right and walked down the bench to chants of "Ste-vie! Ste-vie!"

In August, Yzerman underwent a radical knee realignment procedure called an osteotomy. Instead of spending his days playing and leading, he was undergoing rehabilitation. With luck, his career might continue. With more luck, he might return by February.

"I felt out of place," Yzer-man said.

For the ceremony's grand finale, a smoke-like substance gushed down from the Jumbotron and the Stanley Cup was revealed at center ice. Sergei Fedorov handed it to his captain. "It wasn't part of the plan," Yzerman said. "They were supposed to carry it, but they said they wanted me to do it."

He led a pied-piper parade across the ice until the championship team was gathered, and they stood clustered as the banner was raised. "I thought it was great," Yzerman said. "I enjoyed seeing the Cup, and raising the banner was nice."

Hasek found his name on the Cup. It was a first. He beamed.

Yzerman finally retired in 2006. Bowman never coached again but he kept acquiring championship rings, first as a consultant with the Wings and then with the Blackhawks working with his son Stan.

Like a cigarette smoker kept trying to quit, Hasek retired and unretired every few years. He returned to the Wings in 2003-04 but a groin injury limited him to 14 games. He returned again and was the starter in 2006-07 and 2007-08. The latter team won his second Stanley Cup, but Hasek struggled early in the playoffs and Chris Osgood went between the pipes the rest of the way. In 2010-11, at age 46, Hasek played 46 games for Spartak Moscow in the KHL. He posted a 2.48 goals-against average and seven shutouts. His induction to the Hockey Hall of Fame came in 2014.

Out of uniform

Because of knee surgery two months prior, Steve Yzerman found himself in street clothes for his third banner-raising ceremony. His teammates insisted that he carry the Stanley Cup even though he couldn't skate with it.

JULIAN H. GONZALEZ/DETROIT FREE PRESS

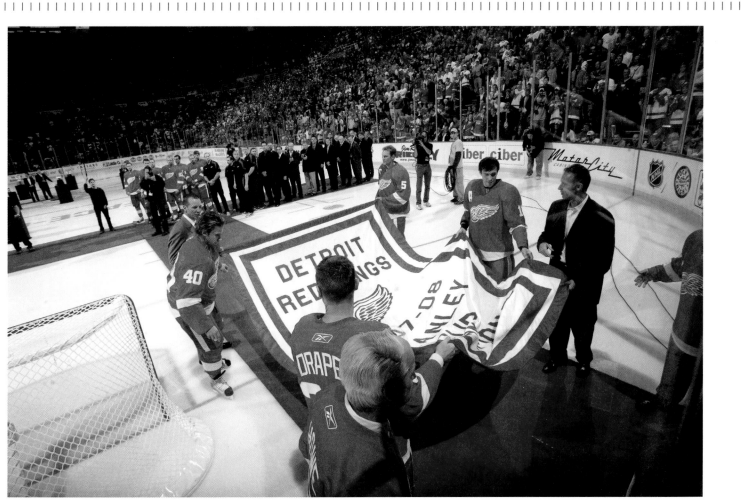

One more time

Captain Nicklas Lidstrom (No. 5) and alternates Henrik Zetterberg (No. 40), Kris Draper (No. 33) and Pavel Datsyuk (No. 13) straighten out the championship banner before its ride to the roof. "Guys see the banner go up," goalie Chris Osgood said, "and it's an honor for us."
JULIAN H. GONZALEZ/DETROIT FREE PRESS

NO. 17: OCT. 9, 2008

11TH OURS

OLD AND NEW RED WINGS UNITE FOR ANOTHER BANNER-RAISING CEREMONY

The old guard delivered the banner to the new guard, the grizzled champions meeting the fresh ones on the ice.

The full richness of the Red Wings' fabled hockey empire bloomed in red and white at The Joe. The 2008 champions were crowned again, this time with a banner that made a long, slow, spot-lit journey from the ice to the rafters to celebrate the franchise's 11th Stanley Cup.

The banner was brought out by Production Line II alums Gordie Howe, Ted Lindsay and Alex Delvecchio and former Wings Johnny Wilson, Dennis Hextall and Doug Brown. Captain Nicklas Lidstrom also grabbed hold, as did his three alternates — Pavel Datsyuk, Kris Draper and Henrik Zetterberg.

"That was special to see the old play-

ers, the former players come out for the celebration and handing over the banner to the current players," Lidstrom said. "It was enjoyable and fun to be a part of."

As the ceremony began, there were big cheers for general manager Ken Holland, the man who put the team together, and his assistant, Jim Nill, the man who helped uncover draft gems like Datsyuk and Zetterberg, and for vice president and former captain Steve Yzerman, who was with the players for the previous three banner raisings.

Lidstrom led the parade of current players, who were introduced one by one. Chris Chelios, at 46 older than his coach, got a rousing greeting, as did Chris Osgood, who left Detroit only to

come back a better goalie.

Dominik Hasek and Dallas Drake took a day off from retirement for one last trip onto the ice. "An emotional day," Hasek said. "It was a very special moment. … I made a good decision to say good-bye to the NHL."

On the ice, forming a circle around the winged logo, was the hardware from the season: Zetterberg's Conn Smythe Trophy, Lidstrom's Norris Trophy, Datsyuk's Selke and Lady Byng trophies. Then Lidstrom brought out the biggest and baddest trophy of all, the Stanley Cup, setting off flashes from cameras and phones through the sold-out stands.

"It's important we enjoy the celebration," coach Mike Babcock said, "but the celebration is all about last year."

NO. 18: MARCH 6, 2014
HIGH FIVE!
WITH NO. 9 TAKEN, LIDSTROM'S NO. 5 BANNER JOINS THE ROW OF LEGENDS

Before his No. 5 jersey rose to the rafters, Nicklas Lidstrom revealed to fans that he had asked to wear No. 9 because that's "what I wore in Sweden." Told by the Red Wings that "kid, that ain't gonna happen," Lidstrom said from then on he focused on "keeping my mouth shut."

Lidstrom called it "a tremendous honor" to see his jersey join the company of Gordie Howe's No. 9, plus Steve Yzerman's No. 19, Sid Abel's No. 12, Alex Delvecchio's No. 10, Ted Lindsay's No. 7 and Terry Sawchuk's No. 1, a legend's row of banners.

Lidstrom had retired in May 2012 with hardware and history galore after two decades with the Wings. Four Stanley Cup championships. Seven Norris trophies as the NHL's best defenseman. The first European player selected MVP of the playoffs. The first European-born and –trained captain to win the Cup. Membership in the Triple Gold Club: Olympic gold medal, World Championship gold medal, Stanley Cup champion.

He had another great night at The Joe:

▶ The first catch-in-your-throat moment came when Vladimir Konstantinov was introduced to chants of "Vlad-die! Vlad-die! Vlad-die!" The fans stood, his former teammates stood, he stood — and everyone wondered what might have been if Konstantinov and Lidstrom could have played together longer.

▶ The night drew a great collection of former Wings, including Brendan Shanahan, Scotty Bowman, Igor Larinov, Chris Chelios, Mark Howe, Delvecchio and Lindsay. Yzerman didn't make it because his duties in Tampa Bay were rather hectic after the trade deadline.

▶ Lidstrom and his family walked out between two lines of current Wings who had donned No. 5 jerseys. Unfortunately, two Wings were in street clothes: Henrik Zetterberg and Pavel Datsyuk.

▶ Lidstrom was introduced to a standing ovation of nearly a minute and a half. He got nice parting gifts, too: a Ram truck from the club — "It will be a great ride back in Sweden," he said — and a family trip for an African safari from the players.

▶ If tears were shed, it didn't look like Lidstrom shed them. He was obviously proud, honored and touched, but as calm, cool and collected as ever.

▶ Mike Babcock, the first speaker, said: "I had the opportunity to coach Nick starting in '05-06 and I coached him for seven years. Many people think he coached me."

▶ Babcock again: "As good a player as he was, he was a better man and a better teammate. Beyond humble, no maintenance, led by example, did it right every day."

▶ Christopher Ilitch, pinch hitting for parents Mike and Marian, noted Lidstrom's nickname, The Perfect Human: "But my parents, and our hockey club, we could have a nickname for Nick, too: a perfect Red Wing."

▶ Lidstrom thanked many people — the Ilitches, Yzerman, fans, former coaches and teammates, his Swedish buddy Tomas Holmstrom — and had a special salute for his family: "It's just not my name, it's our name on the back of my sweater."

Before the ceremony, Shanahan summed up Lidstrom perfectly. "You always say it's a game of mistakes," he said, "but Nick proved us all wrong."

‹‹ Magnificent Seven

With the retirement of Nicklas Lidstrom's No. 5, seven jersey banners hung from The Joe's rafters: No. 1 — Terry Sawchuk, retired March 6, 1994. No. 7 — Ted Lindsay, retired Nov. 10, 1991. No. 9 — Gordie Howe, retired March 12, 1972. No. 10 — Alex Delvecchio, retired Nov. 10, 1991. No. 12 — Sid Abel, retired April 29, 1995. No. 19 — Steve Yzerman, retired Jan. 2, 2007.

DIANE WEISS/DETROIT FREE PRESS

The Perfect Human

Nicklas Lidstrom and his family walked the red carpet covering the ice while his former teammates honored him by donning No. 5 Lidstrom jerseys. General manager Ken Holland, though, had a lament: "Boy, do I miss watching No. 5 play."

DIANE WEISS/DETROIT FREE PRESS

Family viewing

Nicklas Lidstrom watched his No. 5 rise to the rafters with his wife, Annika, and their sons, Kevin, Adam, Samuel and Lucas. In his remarks during the ceremony, Lidstrom praised his family: "It's just not my name, it's our name on the back of my sweater." Lidstrom retired in 2012 and his jersey would have been retired in 2013 but an NHL lockout pushed it back a year.

JULIAN H. GONZALEZ/DFP

OPEN HOUSE

**WINGS CHRISTEN THEIR
NEW RIVERFRONT HOME
WITHOUT JOE LOUIS BUT
WITH A BLOWN LEAD**

After 52 years of pro hockey at Olympia Stadium, the Red Wings moved into Joe Louis Arena, their new but not-really-finished riverfront arena. The team also had trouble finishing, as it blew a third-period lead and lost to the St. Louis Blues, 3-2. "We gave it away," general manager Ted Lindsay lamented.

The 19,742 fans, who set an attendance record for Motor City hockey, were fired up but booed each time the announcer mentioned the arena's name. They didn't have anything against Joe Louis, the legendary heavyweight boxing champion from Detroit; they were upset that the Wings had left beloved Olympia, the prices went up, the lines for the restrooms and concession stands were ridiculous, and there were other perceived and real slights.

The arena's name was selected when teams and cities didn't know to squeeze out extra bucks by selling corporate sponsors the naming rights. The Detroit City Council, legally empowered to name public facilities in the city, decided in June 1978 to honor a request from the Committee to Honor Joe Louis, a group of citizens.

"He is seriously ill and now his days are numbered," committee spokeswoman Mary Clavon told the city council.

Clavon had visited Louis, 64, recently in Las Vegas and said he barely could speak and showed little emotion. But she said he was very moved when told the arena might be named after him. Asked whether he would come to a dedication ceremony, he replied: "I will be there, God willing."

In the unanimously approved resolution, the council said "the naming of a major downtown center is an appropriate tribute to the dignity, courage and commitment that Joe Louis symbolizes." His sister, Vunice Barrow High, attended the council vote and called the naming of the new sports arena "a beautiful, fitting tribute." But she also said "we should have done something years ago."

Louis' health never improved. He never returned to Detroit. He died in April 1981, with his funeral in a casino sports arena and burial in Arlington National Ceremony. The Joe's dedication ceremony finally was held in October 1983.

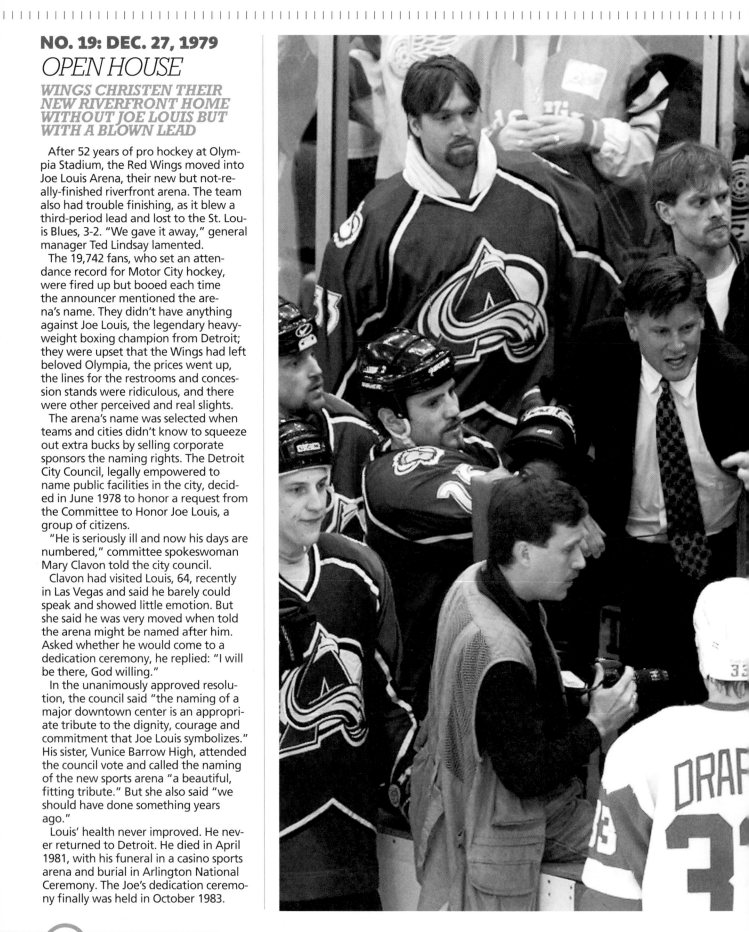

A BLOWUP IN A BLOWOUT

BOWMAN VS. CRAWFORD: AVALANCHE COACH CLIMBS THE GLASS, EARNS BIG FINE

When the Red Wings and Avalanche said they didn't like each other, they really meant it. And Game 4 of the 1997 Western Conference finals, a 6-0 Wings victory for a three-games-to-one series lead, proved the coaches didn't like each other, either.

While the players scuffled on the ice in the third period, for a combined 204 penalty minutes, the coaches engaged in a shouting match on the benches. With 2:18 left, Colorado's Marc Crawford climbed the glass to the photographers' well that separated the benches and screamed at Detroit's Scotty Bowman. A linesman scaled the boards to get between the verbal contestants.

"He was pretty emotional," Bowman said. "I told him, 'It's a game, it's over, there's about two minutes left.' His eyes were coming out of his head. So he was pretty excited."

Bowman also calmly told Crawford: "I knew your father before you did, and I don't think he'd be too proud of what you're doing right now."

Crawford offered this explanation: "It was nothing. I said some stupid things, and he said some stupid things. We got caught up in the emotion. It's part of the game."

The next day Bowman reconsidered his statement whether Floyd Crawford would have been proud of his son's behavior. "Then again,"

Bowman said, "maybe he would be, because he's a competitor."

Bowman remembered Floyd Crawford from his junior days in Belleville, Ontario. "His father was an ultra-competitor," he said. "He played a lot like (Vladimir) Konstantinov. He hated to lose, and he didn't give an inch. The Crawfords are tough people."

Among the penalties in the final period were eight fighting majors, 10 misconducts, three game misconducts, two instigating penalties and one goalie interference, while the puck was in the neutral zone (thanks, Rene Corbet).

The bloodiest battle? When Brendan Shanahan roughed up Corbet. Shanahan bled from friendly fire (an errant Martin Lapointe stick). Corbet, holding a towel to the back of his head, needed two people to help him to the bench.

When the teams weren't fighting, the Wings got two-goal performances from playmaker Igor Larinov and grinder Kirk Maltby, who had three in the entire regular season.

The NHL socked Crawford with a $10,000 fine. He finally offered an apology: "I embarrassed the league, and more important I embarrassed my team. And for that, I am sorry. There's no way you can justify anything like that. If you try to, it's wrong. I was wrong."

Let's go crazy

In the third period of Game 4, the Avalanche racked up 100 minutes in penalties and coach Marc Crawford made an attempt to get at Wings players and coaches after several minutes of screaming. "You say some things and they say some things," Crawford said. "Things got out of hand. ... Nobody is proud of it." The Red Wings were so furious about the Avalanche's attempts to intimidate them that after the game they spoke stoically or not at all to the media. "I've got nothing to say," said Darren McCarty, one of the league's most talkative players. "You guys watched the game. Report what you saw."
JULIAN H. GONZALEZ/DETROIT FREE PRESS

NO. 21: DEC. 26, 1996
HIGH FIVE FOR SERGEI!
FEDOROV SCORES FIVE TIMES, INCLUDING THE WINNER IN OVERTIME

Amazing fact No. 1: Sergei Fedorov scored all five goals, including the winner with 2:21 left in overtime, as the Red Wings beat Washington, 5-4, at The Joe on the night after Christmas.

Amazing fact No. 2: Fedorov's performance did not merit a story on the front page of the Free Press sports section the next day.

For Fedorov, it was his first five-goal night, second four-goal night and third career hat trick. Only one Wing had done better: Syd Howe with six goals against the Rangers on Feb. 3, 1944.

For the Free Press, Fedorov didn't make the sports front because all the stories dealt with Lions coach Wayne Fontes. The headline said it all: "The Buck stops here." After nine rollercoaster seasons, William Clay Ford Sr. finally fired Fontes. He had survived long enough to become the winningest and losingest coach in franchise history.

At the beginning of the hockey season, Fedorov couldn't buy a goal. He had one in the first 11 games. But he had been on a tear since the Russian Five of Fedorov, Igor Larionov, Slava Kozlov, Vladimir Konstantinov and Slava Fetisov, once beset by injuries, had regained its health and was reunited by coach Scotty Bowman.

"He had a lot of quality chances," Konstantinov said, "but he didn't score. He didn't believe in himself. … I told him if he can believe in himself, he can score goals."

Against the Caps, Fedorov scored at 7:32 of the first period (Wings, 1-0), 3:46 of the second (Wings, 2-1), 10:33 of the third (3-3), 12:08 of the third (4-4) and 2:39 of overtime (Wings, 5-4). Konstantinov assisted on four of Fedorov's goals, Larionov on three and Fetisov on one.

Fedorov also scored four times in a 4-4 tie with Los Angeles on Feb. 12, 1995. He missed a penalty shot in overtime that would have won it. Against the Capitals, there was no such flaw. When he fired a drop pass from Konstantinov past goalie Jim Carey, The Joe exploded.

"This night was like rolling stones from the mountain coming at me," Fedorov said. "I was very excited, because the overtime goal, that's the most exciting part of the game."

NO. 22: NOV. 21, 2005
FISCHER'S FALL
TIME STANDS STILL AFTER THE DEFENSEMAN'S COLLAPSE

"His heart had stopped, and there was no pulse. But they hooked up the auto defibrillator, and they shocked him. The heartbeat that leads to death, they got that stopped, and going, and they continued with the CPR."

As he delivered those words, Red Wings coach Mike Babcock looked shaken, like his team, the rest of The Joe and the rest of Wings Nation after D-man Jiri Fischer collapsed on the bench midway through the first period against Nashville.

But Babcock concluded with the best news of the night: "It's our understanding that things are fine, and that he is going to be fine. He's stable."

The most frightening incident in The Joe's history began around 8:07 p.m. The Predators just had taken a 1-0 lead at 11:28, and play had resumed. Fischer, only 25, was seated on the far end of the bench when he fell to the ground, right by the door the Wings used to get on and off the ice. Babcock immediately stepped onto the bench and waved his arms toward the Zamboni entrance, where the ambulance was stationed. Assistant coach Todd McClellan went over to Fischer, and soon handfuls of players gathered around, too. A whistle was blown at 12:30, halting play. The game would never resume.

"Fisch was out on a shift, he came off, he was standing there with his teammates, or sitting on the bench, and he had a seizure," Babcock said.

Team doctor Anthony Colucci, sitting right behind the bench in the stands, immediately jumped down and began administering CPR. Team doctor Douglas Plagens and trainer Piet Van Zant also tended to Fischer.

Soon after the collapse, most of the Wings and the Predators retreated to their locker rooms. Yzerman, Brendan Shanahan, Kris Draper and Robert Lang, a Czech like Fischer, stayed on the ice, hovering over their fallen teammate.

At one point, Shanahan and Lang skated to the Zamboni entrance and helped Fischer's finacee, Avery, to his side. At

CONTINUED ON PAGE 67

Teammate down

Coach Mike Babcock helped to clear the area as medical personnel tried to save the life of defenseman Jiri Fischer after he collapsed.

JULIAN H. GONZALEZ/DETROIT FREE PRESS

CONTINUED FROM PAGE 66

another point, Yzerman and Shanahan skated a stretcher to the bench, and fans cheered a few minutes after it appeared the crisis was over. But they fell silent after no one was loaded onto the stretcher and it was taken away.

Shanahan and Babcock said Fischer looked fine before the game. Babcock said reviews of the game tape gave no indication something was wrong before Fischer's collapse.

However, Fischer had an abnormal EKG during training camp in 2002. He later passed follow-up tests. "There is a little abnormality," Fischer said then, "but nothing that will stop me from playing." He added that his heart was a little thicker than normal.

Fischer spent the night at Detroit Receiving Hospital. By the next day, doctors knew only that Fischer's heart fell into a terminal rhythm, which meant the muscle wasn't beating in an organized manner and was unable to pump blood back into the body. Soon after, Fischer went home.

Doctors eventually determined that Fischer should never play pro hockey again but he likely could live a long life. He moved right into the front office. He played again — but only in alumni games.

NO. 23: FEB. 4, 1994
FIGHT NIGHT AT THE JOE
PROBERT, MCSORLEY ROCK 'EM AND SOCK 'EM

Bob Probert, the NHL's reigning heavyweight champion, and Marty McSorley, a bruiser for the Penguins, engaged in a titanic display of fisticuffs that hockey fight fans consider one of the best slugfests in the sport's history — and possibly its longest example of sustained combat.

The nearly two-minute exchange of blows between Probert, listed at 6-feet-3, 225 pounds, and McSorley, listed at 6-1, 235, ended evenly with 19,875 fans at The Joe on their feet, roaring their approval.

"That's the best fight I've ever seen," Wings forward Ray Sheppard said. "It had to give both teams a good feeling, as far as momentum, but it also gave everybody a bit of amazement, too. They were throwing punches to kill each other."

Probert asked for the dance and McSorley accepted without hesitation at 13:04 of the first period. What followed left both fighters dazed and exhausted as they skated slowly to the penalty boxes to a thunderous standing ovation.

Probert, connecting on a variety of early punches, knocked McSorley off his skates and pulled him up to hit him some more. But McSorley took everything Probert threw at him and had the stamina to counterattack with heavy punches late in the bout that knocked Probert against the boards.

"I really think the linesman and the referee did a great job," McSorley said. "They yelled several times, 'Want us to come in?' And both Bob and I kept saying, 'Get out of here!'"

The combatants escaped relatively unharmed. Probert opened an old cut to the side of McSorley's left eye. McSorley reopened a cut on Probert's left ear.

"It's one of the longest ones I've ever had," Probert said. "I know it was the most tired I've ever been after a fight."

McSorley countered: "I've got a lot of respect for Bob Probert. He always stands up for his team, and he puts a lot of pounds on a lot of players."

While the McSorley bout might have been the best of Probert's distinguished pugilistic career among hockey fight aficionados, the most famous among Wings fans occurred in New York's Madison Square Garden.

On Feb. 9, 1992, Probert couldn't resist repeated invitations by the Rangers' Tie Domi. Probert hadn't fought since Jan. 3 against Toronto's Craig Berube. Against

Domi, listed at 5-10, 215, Probert would need four stitches near his right eye, but he left Domi dazed with two hard rights to the head before officials intervened. "I'll get him better in Detroit," Probert vowed.

As he wobbled to the penalty box, Domi mocked Probert's reputation as the NHL's heavyweight champ by motioning with his hands across his waist as if wearing a championship belt. "Macho Man Savage does that," Domi said. "It's a WWF thing. I was real excited. … When I saw the blood, I was kind of happy."

Probert countered: "The little dummy. He wanted a shot at the title, and he got it. If he wants to wear the belt, let him. More power to him. I'm here to play hockey."

Domi was injured when the Rangers came to The Joe the next month.

"Regrets? Yeah, that's part of the game, paybacks," Probert said. "But I know what number he wears. Maybe we'll see him in the playoffs. If not, then next year — if he makes the team."

The rematch wouldn't come until the next season, again in the Big Apple, on Dec. 3, 1992. Domi had been hyping the fight for weeks, drawing public reprimands from NHL president Gil Stein and Rangers GM Neil Smith.

But it was Probert who pressed the issue when they were on the ice for a face-off 30 seconds into the game. The puck was dropped and, after about a minute of furious swinging, so was Domi. Probert outpunched his vocal adversary, 47-21, for a victory so decisive that Wings coach Bryan Murray asked, "Was it a fight?"

Domi appeared to land a couple punches early, none of which fazed his much taller and heavier opponent. But Probert scored with many of his punches, two of which truly hurt Domi. One knocked him down and the next quickly followed with Domi on the ice as officials intervened. Probert skated directly to the penalty box. Domi arose a moment later, then began smiling and waving to the crowd during a slow skate to the box.

"He could have hit me a thousand times; it didn't matter to me," Domi said, admitting that Probert was still the champ. "Look at the size of that guy. … I'm a small guy, but I show up."

As for Probert, he said little after the rematch. "I did my talking," he told reporters, "on the ice."

Sid's place of honor

In 1995, the Red Wings finally retired Sid Abel's No. 12. As it went to the rafters, Ted Lindsay's No. 7 and Gordie Howe's No. 9 moved in opposite directions to make room for their center. In 2000, after Abel's death, his banner was lowered briefly and then returned to be with his linemates. Although the Wings retired No. 12, Abel actually wore several numbers: 4, 7, 9, 11, 12, 14, 19 and 20.

JULIAN H. GONZALEZ/DETROIT FREE PRESS

NO. 24: APRIL 29, 1995
PRODUCTION LINE REUNION
JERSEY NUMBERS OF HOWE, LINDSAY AND ABEL FINALLY HANG FROM THE JOE'S RAFTERS

Nearly 60 years after his Red Wings debut, Sid Abel's No. 12 jersey finally was retired and raised to The Joe's rafters.

As Abel, 77 at the time, stood on the red carpet with his family, his banner slowly rose from ice level before a packed house for a Saturday matinee. And then — give PR director Bill Jamieson credit for this idea — Ted Lindsay's No. 7 moved slowly to the left while Gordie Howe's No. 9 slid over the right, making room for their center on perhaps the most famous trio in NHL history. At last, for eternity, the original Production Line was back together.

The Ilitch family did the right thing, but they got a nudge from the public. It was before social media, so the team's fax machine was flooded with pleas from fans to retire the number of one of the most beloved Wings: captain, coach, general manager, broadcaster, MVP, Hall of Famer. He served the club in so many capacities for most of the half-century from the late 1930s to the late 1980s.

After the ceremony, the Wings beat the Dallas Stars, 4-2, to clinch the Presidents' Trophy, awarded to the team with the most points, a feat Detroit accomplished seven times in the 1950s but only in 1964-65 afterward. During

the Dead Wings era of the early '80s, Abel, although the color analyst on radio broadcasts, might well have been the organization's most popular figure. Fans appreciated his honesty on broadcasts and loved to mimic his western Canada accent and speech patterns. "Detroit are skating well tonight," Abel would say.

In 1950, when Abel won his second Stanley Cup in Detroit, Lindsay (78 points), Abel (69) and Howe (68) finished 1-2-3 in league scoring. Upon Abel's death in February 2000, the Wings held a moment of silence and briefly lowered his No. 12 from its honored position.

"It's just a tremendous loss," Howe said. "It'll be a long time trying to forget that guy." Lindsay added: "When close friends like that go, you move one row closer to the front of the church."

Next Hall of Famer?

At the time, the 2001-02 Red Wings figured to have nine Hall of Fame locks: Chris Chelios, Sergei Fedorov, Dominik Hasek, Brett Hull, Igor Larionov, Nicklas Lidstrom, Luc Robitaille, Brendan Shanahan and Steve Yzerman. Indeed, everyone was inducted into the Hockey Hall of Fame by 2015. Will Pavel Datsyuk make it double digits? He was a rookie in 2001-02, centering a line with Hull and Boyd Devereaux. After 14 seasons in Detroit, a homesick Datsyuk returned to Russia following the 2015-16 season. His resume: three Selke trophies, four Lady Byng trophies, 314 goals and 604 assists for 918 points in 953 games.

JULIAN H. GONZALEZ/DETROIT FREE PRESS

NO. 25: JAN. 9, 2002
DAT'S A GREAT ONE!
DAZZLING RUSSIAN ROOKIE CRAFTS THE PLAY OF THE YEAR

Mired in a midseason funk of fumbling late leads, the Red Wings turned an almost certain defeat into a defining moment for the "Hockey Gods" and Russian rookie Pavel Datsyuk.

Coming off a three-day break in the schedule, the Wings nonetheless were sluggish and trailed Vancouver, 3-0 after the first period and 4-1 after the second. Then a shot by Steve Yzerman hit Brendan Shanahan and went into the goal. Less than a minute later, Datsyuk made the season's prettiest play, an end-to-end rush through three Canucks. "Just a beautiful goal," Yzerman said. When Datsyuk set up Brett Hull's tying goal, The Joe went insane. Kris Draper won it in overtime, 5-4.

When Budd Lynch announced the three stars, Datsyuk, a rookie, a baby on what was supposed to be an old-timers' team, was No. 1. He took a spin on the ice, strolled into the dressing room and got a big reception from his teammates. "Big smile on his face," linemate Boyd Devereaux said.

In his book, "Hockey Gods," Nicholas J. Cotsonika of the Free Press wrote:

Datsyuk led stretching before and after practice the next day. The honor was his. When reporters came calling, they had to use Maxim Kuznetsov as an interpreter: Datsyuk had been in Detroit only about four months and the Russian spoke little English. Still they found he had plenty of savvy and a sense of humor.

"What about the game?" a reporter asked.

"He's forgotten game already," Kuznetsov said. "He's preparing for next game."

"Why did he come over to the NHL?"

"He say they fire him in Russia," Kuznetsov said, smiling. "He's joking."

"Who was his favorite player?"

"Max Kuznetsov."

NO. 26: DEC. 18, 1987
COACHES GONE WILD
DEMERS VS. BROOKS: WAR OF WORDS NEARLY BECOMES WAR OF FISTS

Red Wings coach Jacques Demers tried to climb over the boards separating the benches to fight Minnesota North Stars coach Herb Brooks.

The uproar at The Joe began with the scored tied, 3-3, at 10:50 of the middle period. What began as an end-to-end waltz involving every player on the ice except goalies turned into a round of slam dancing with sticks and spilled over to the benches.

Demers and Brooks, best known as the U.S. coach for the "Miracle on Ice" at the 1980 Lake Placid Olympics, began exchanging unkind words. Demers made his move toward the Stars' bench, fell back trying to scale the boards and then was restrained by assistant coach Don MacAdam and left wing Mel Bridgman as he wildly swung his arms trying to get free. All the while, Brooks smiled and invited Demers over the two-foot gap, but no glass, between the benches by saying, "C'mon. C'mon."

Frustrated, Demers, a fiery French-Canadian, picked up a helmet and tried to throw it at Brooks, but someone behind the Wings' bench knocked it away.

On the Minnesota side, someone grabbed ex-Wing Basil McRae's sweater after he had taken a stride off the bench. Had he gone farther, he likely would have incited the first bench-clearing brawl of the season. The NHL warned before the season it would fine teams $100,000 for such incidents.

Brooks later recalled to Sports Illustrated that he had called Demers a "milk-truck driver" and said, "I told Jacques, 'Jacques, I'll go, but I don't think you can skate.'"

In his profile of a new "mellow" Brooks, SI's Austin Murphy also wrote: "A Detroit player dissolved much of the tension by skating past Brooks and saying out of the corner of his mouth, 'I'm taking you in two.' The North Stars' bench broke up."

Demers, for the record, drove a Coca-Cola delivery truck in Montreal for 11 years.

After a 15-minute delay, the Wings scored five straight en route to an 8-3 victory over their Norris rival. Gerard Gallant recorded the first hat trick of his career.

NO. 27: MARCH 1, 1988

PLEASURE, THEN PAIN

MINUTES AFTER HIS 50TH GOAL, STEVIEY SUFFERS A CAREER-THREATENING INJURY

Early in the second period, Steve Yzerman flicked a backhand past Tom Barrasso, the Buffalo goalie who had edged him for rookie of the year in 1984. The 50th red light of Yzerman's season ignited an incredible roar from the crowd at The Joe.

Coach Jacques Demers applauded from the end of the bench. Yzerman's teammates stood and pounded their gloves on the boards. Yzerman retrieved the puck, skated toward his bench and flung the puck into the crowd.

So much for a keepsake as the fourth Red Wing to reach the 50-goal milestone. Mickey Redmond (twice), Danny Grant and John Ogrodnick had done it, too, but not in 64 games like Yzerman.

Late in the same period, Yzerman chased No. 51. He gathered a loose puck along the left boards and skated in again on Barrasso. As Yzerman cut from left to right, Calle Johansson checked him as Barrasso guarded the right corner of the crease. Suddenly, Yzerman, Johansson and Barrasso collided. "He might have stepped on my stick," Johansson, a rookie, said. "I was behind him and he just seemed to go down." The left post stopped Yzerman's slide. Barrasso said Yzerman's right knee didn't appear to hit the anchored post very hard, "but he hit it at a bad angle."

With Yzerman writhing in pain and the training staff racing on the ice, the boisterous crowd turned silent and still. The Wings' front office, coaches and players were equally devastated, "in shock," according to Demers. "That's fate," the coach said. "I believe in fate, and it came true."

The Wings announced after the game that Yzerman would have reconstructive knee surgery the following day and miss 12-18 months. But owner Mike Ilitch ordered a second opinion or a third or a fourth to determine the best course of action. Instead of a major operation and a long recovery, Yzerman had his knee scoped and worked overtime to strength the muscles around it. A mere nine weeks later, he played in the Campbell Conference finals against Edmonton.

NO. 28: FEB. 24, 2003

CAPTAIN COMEBACK

ONCE AGAIN, YZERMAN SHOWS THAT HE'S ALL HEART

The official word came after the pregame warm-ups: He was playing. He was back. Steve Yzerman, the captain, the mayor of Hockeytown, whose giant image was being painted on the Cadillac Tower in the heart of the city, was making an unprecedented return from knee realignment surgery.

For the most part, fans at The Joe remained silent as Yzerman stood by the bench for the national anthem, but then they roared. And when he hopped off the bench 54 seconds into the first period, centering Boyd Devereaux and Luc Robitaille, just wanting lineman Ray Scapinello to drop the puck quickly so that he could get going, the fans rose to their feet and roared again.

"Stev-ie!" they chanted. "Stev-ie!" Scapinello stepped back to allow the applause a few extra seconds. "I was thinking," Yzerman would say later, smiling, "that Ray should drop the puck."

Yzerman shook off eight months of rust as the game progressed. He played 13:17 — 3:46 in the first period, 5:22 in the second and 4:09 in the third. He skated with different linemates, sometimes at center, sometimes at right wing. He took no shots and had no points, but he was plus-1 and won nine of 15 face-offs, the last in his zone with 23.8 seconds left and the Wings protecting a 5-4 lead over the Kings.

"I really enjoyed being back out on the ice," Yzerman said. "I felt actually better than I expected."

He hadn't played since June 13, 2002. The Wings won the Stanley Cup that night, and during the commotion, while the confetti still was failing, he said, "What do you think would happen if I announced my retirement right now?"

It would have been a fitting finale to a Hall of Fame career: In a matter of months, he had won an Olympic gold medal for Canada and his third Cup for the Wings, and he had done it at age 37 despite unspeakable hardship. His right knee was wrecked. He tore his posterior cruciate ligament in 1988 and didn't have it reconstructed. He wore away his cartilage over the years until bone ground against bone. Two games into the playoffs, the Wings weren't sure he could go on — but he went on, leading them on and off the ice, although he needed constant treatment, took countless injections, had trouble scaling the steps up to the team plane and hardly left his home or hotel room. Walking hurt. Even standing hurt. The knee ached all the time.

"He's a freak of nature," trainer John Wharton said. "I think he has a different nervous system than the rest of us. I don't think he processes pain."

Later in the summer, Yzerman underwent an osteotomy, a procedure that realigned the knee to redistribute weight, a procedure usually performed on the elderly with degenerative bone disease, a procedure that never had been done on a professional athlete.

"It came down to what was the best thing for my knee, No. 1," Yzerman said, "and then what's going to give me the best chance of playing again."

He appeared in 15 more games during the regular season, scoring eight points, and won the Masterton Trophy for perseverance, sportsmanship and dedication. He played 75 games with 51 points the following season and, after a lockout canceled the 2004-05 season, played 61 games with 34 points at age 40 in his final season.

On the night of his emotional 2003 return, columnist Mitch Albom wrote for the Free Press: "'Stevie When?' is 'Steve Y' again. The skeptics are shaken. The surgeons are baffled. The medical world says you don't have this operation and return to chase a Stanley Cup. But when doctors chart an osteotomy, the first thing they do is draw a line from the ankles to the hips. And that was their mistake. With Yzerman, they should have drawn it to his heart."

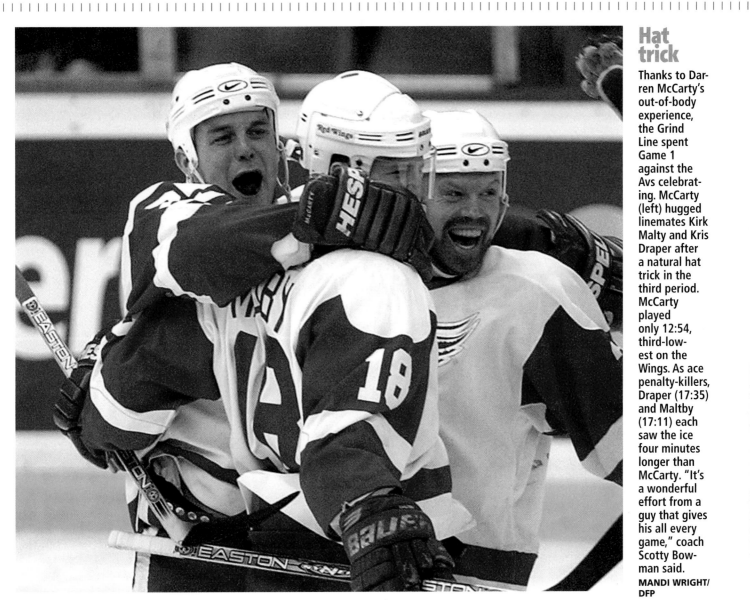

Thanks to Darren McCarty's out-of-body experience, the Grind Line spent Game 1 against the Avs celebrating. McCarty (left) hugged linemates Kirk Malty and Kris Draper after a natural hat trick in the third period. McCarty played only 12:54, third-lowest on the Wings. As ace penalty-killers, Draper (17:35) and Maltby (17:11) each saw the ice four minutes longer than McCarty. "It's a wonderful effort from a guy that gives his all every game," coach Scotty Bowman said.
MANDI WRIGHT/ DFP

NO. 29: MAY 18, 2002
BIG MAC ATTACK
APOCALYPSE NOW? MCCARTY'S SUDDEN SCORING OUTBURST CATCHES AVS BY SURPRISE

His first goal was cheered.

His second one was greeted by wild applause and a lone octopus.

His third one left the ice at The Joe littered with hats and octopi, real and man-made, as 20,058 fans erupted in a party.

The production was as much a surprise to the Colorado Avalanche as to the delighted scorer. After five goals in 62 regular-season games, Red Wings forward Darren McCarty pulled off a natural hat trick in less than 15 third-period minutes to carry Detroit to a 5-3 victory in Game 1 of the 2002 Western Conference finals.

"You've all read the Bible and heard of the Apocalypse?" McCarty said, his big smile highlighting a missing front tooth. "It's my first hat trick. It's huge."

Besides end-of-time biblical events, left wing Luc Robitaille and former teammate Joe Kocur played a role in McCarty's sudden scoring outburst. Robitaille picked out a stick for McCarty, who said Kocur, the team's video coordinator, then put "a voodoo hex" on it.

In the second period, McCarty tried to hit Rob Blake only to wind up writhing on the ice when Blake's stick speared him in the groin. "That's not a good feeling," McCarty said. "Those things happen."

With the game tied at 2, McCarty scored for the first time in playoffs 1:18 into the third period when Patrick Roy misjudged his shot, scored again at 12:44 on a slap shot from the right circle that few over Roy's left shoulder, and scored one more time when he fired in Kirk Maltby's rebound at 15:55.

"They were all great goals against one of the greatest goaltenders who ever played the game," coach Scotty Bowman said. "There wasn't anything lucky about any of them."

Roy agreed: "I played good."

Still, he was subjected to "Pa-trick!" taunts after each goal and numerous "Ha-sek's bet-ter!" chants from the fans with Stanley Cup fever.

Sorry, Sid

Red Wings goalie Chris Osgood slammed the door on Pittsburgh's Sidney Crosby in the first period of Game 2. Osgood made 22 saves while posting his second straight shutout in the Stanley Cup finals. Afterward, the Penguins were irked at Osgood — for his acting. Forwards Ryan Malone and Petr Sykora received penalties for goaltender interference. "I reviewed those plays," Pittsburgh coach Michel Therrien said. "He is a good actor. He goes to players, and he's diving. … I know our players are frustrated right now." Osgood replied: "I've been called worse."

MANDI WRIGHT/
DETROIT FREE PRESS

Nowhere to turn

Pittsburgh's Marian Hossa couldn't find room to maneuver against a sprawling Chris Osgood in Game 1. Osgood had to stop only 19 shots for that shutout. Hossa joined the Wings the following season.
MANDI WRIGHT/DETROIT FREE PRESS

NO. 30: MAY 26, 2008

OSGOOD FILES

WITH SECOND STRAIGHT SHUTOUT OF PENGUINS, OZZIE POSITIONS WINGS FOR THEIR 11TH CUP

"This is the Motor City, and the Red Wings are playing as if right off the line with the pedal to the metal. They have cruised through two games with barely a blemish, barely a nick, seven goals to the positive, none to the negative. Two shutouts? Really? We know they are supposed to be playing a great team out there. The question is, does Pittsburgh know it?"

With these words Free Press columnist Mitch Albom summarized the state of the Stanley Cup finals after Games 1 and 2 at The Joe. Chris Osgood had posted 4-0 and 3-0 shutouts, the 12th and 13th of his career, breaking Terry Sawchuk's team record. Brad Stuart and Tomas Holmstrom had scored in the first period of Game 2. And NHL research had revealed that teams winning the first two games had won the Cup 30 of 31 times.

"They have so many skilled players," captain Nicklas Lidstrom said, "but Ozzie has been coming up big for us."

The series quickly tightened when it moved to Pittsburgh, with each team winning a one-goal game. Back at The Joe, the Penguins stayed alive thanks to a 4-3 Game 5 victory, with Maxim Talbot tying it with 35 seconds left in

regulation, Marc-Andre Fleury making 55 saves and Petr Sykora winning it on the power play in the third overtime.

In Game 6 at Pittsburgh, the Wings built a 3-1 lead as Fleury let in a couple of softies, including one he pushed in with his rump. But the Penguins' Marian Hossa scored a power-play goal with 1:27 left and Sidney Crosby launched a final shot that had kill all over it. Osgood stopped it with his glove, pushed it with his stick just far enough away from Hossa, and as the blue light swirled to mark the end of the game, he was flat on the ice.

"They always have to go right to the bitter end," Osgood said. "I've got a bigger heart than people think."

The Swedes stole the rest of the show: Henrik Zetterberg won the Conn Smythe Trophy as the playoff MVP. Lidstrom became the first European-trained captain to hoist the Cup.

Ken Kal couldn't call the game on radio because of laryngitis, but he took over for Ken Daniels for the final seconds. "Osgood the save and the rebound. … Time will run out, and the Detroit Red Wings are the Stanley Cup champion."

For the 11th time overall and fourth time during the Joe Louis Arena era.

Raise the roof

Reserve goalie Kevin Hodson made raising the roof all the rage among the Wings and their fans. The move had been around for a couple of years, but Hodson introduced to it to the team when celebrating goals in locker-room soccer games. "When Stevie won the Cup, he did a little 'raise the roof' to the guys," Hodson said. "It was personal thing. Everybody knew what it meant." And the fans figured it out quickly.

GABRIEL B. TAIT/DETROIT FREE PRESS

NO. 31: JUNE 9, 1997

ONE MORE YEAR!

AT RALLY, YZERMAN POURS OUT HIS SOUL AND ASKS FANS TO MAKE UP FOR BOOING BOWMAN

To celebrate their first Stanley Cup in 42 years, the night before their parade in downtown Detroit, the Red Wings held a rally at The Joe for season-ticket holders and allowed Channel 50 to broadcast it.

At times, the 2½-hour rally was highly emotional and very amusing; at others, it was slow and almost boring, like the Academy Awards show at its worst. The fans in the half-empty arena were participants in the festivities, including loud chats of "One more year! One more year!" for coach Scotty Bowman and center Igor Larionov.

"We did this for ourselves, for Stevie, for the Ilitches, but we also did this for the City of Detroit and Red Wings fans everywhere," forward Darren McCarty told the crowd, building to his crescendo. "Now, when people say '1955,' they know where to shove it."

But Steve Yzerman stole the show when he poured out his soul in a 10-minute speech. "In 14 years here in Detroit I played on almost 14 different teams, it seems," The Captain said. "This is the closest group of players, the most unselfish group of players, the hardest-working, most-dedicated team I've ever been a part of."

Then Yzerman recalled the rousing ovation he received during the home opener in 1995, when rumors were swirling that Bowman, also director of player personnel, would trade him. "Scotty Bowman's name was announced at that time as well," Yzerman said, "and his reception was a little different from mine. I think this is a great opportunity to make up for that reception."

The fans did, screaming for Bowman as he stood up, holding back tears, as was Yzerman.

Soon after, the Wings jumped from their seats, lifted Yzerman onto their shoulders and handed their leader the Stanley Cup.

As easy as 1-2-3-4

San Jose goalie Evgeni Nabokov didn't know where to turn to stop Johan Frazen from scoring his third goal in the first period of Game 4. Columnist Michael Rosenberg wrote in the Free Press: "The game was 11 minutes, 16 seconds old. He barely had time to watch a sitcom and used it to write an opera. Some players just seem bigger in the playoffs, and Franzen is one of them. I mean that literally: He looks taller, broader, bigger in every way."

KIRTHMON F. DOZIER/DETROIT FREE PRESS

MULE TRAIN KEEPS ROLLING

FRANZEN RECORDS HAT TRICK IN LESS THAN FOUR MINUTES

Left wing Johan Franzen appeared to score the first three goals in a 2010 second-round elimination game against San Jose. One goal was credited to Todd Bertuzzi instead, and before Franzen even knew it, he scored again. He had scored three straight goals and had been responsible for four in a row. The game was 11 minutes, 16 seconds old.

The first goal at 5:40: Bertuzzi created traffic in front of Evgeni Nabokov. Franzen fired a shot. The shot went in. Apparently it hit Bertuzzi, so Franzen had to settle for an assist.

The second goal at 7:50 (officially, his first): Franzen spun around, reached while he was off-balance and backhanded a shot in.

The third goal at 10:43 (officially, his second): Franzen flicked a wrist shot over Nabokov's glove and into the corner of the goal.

The fourth goal at 11:16 (officially, his third): Henrik Zetterberg carried the puck into the zone, but it bounced up and the Sharks' Dan Boyle knocked it out of the air, accidently sending it right to Franken, who whipped it past Nabokov.

Franzen's three goals in 3:36 were the fastest in the playoffs since Philadelphia's Tim Kerr scored three times in 3:24 in 1985. And Franzen still wasn't done in the Wings' 7-1 Game 4 victory. He recorded his second assist in the middle period and his fourth goal at 7:33 of the third period. His six points broke the team playoff record of five, by Norm Ullman in 1963 and '64 and Steve Yzerman in '96.

Always a prolific playoff scorer, Franzen's confidence had been wavering as the Wings fell into a three-games-to-none deficit against the Sharks, each loss by a 4-3 score. "Goal-wise, yeah," Franzen said. The Mule had a heck of a series in Game 4. "Luck," he said, then laughed. "I don't know. It's nothing different." In his past 49 playoff games, he now had 31 goals.

Back in San Jose for Game 5, Franzen took seven shots and assisted on the Wings' lone tally in a final one-goal heartbreaker, 2-1.

CHEVY DRIVES EPIC COMEBACK

CHEVELDAE'S SHUTOUT STREAK REACHES 118:36; WINGS ESCAPE 3-1 HOLE

After their best regular season in a quarter-century, the rebuilding Red Wings were on the brink of a disheartening first-round playoff exit. They had won the Norris Division with 98 points (their highest total since 1952) and 43 victories (exceeded only by the '51 and '52 teams).

But the Wings lost Games 1 and 2 at The Joe against the lowly Minnesota North Stars. After the Stars won Game 4, 5-4, the Wings were in a three-games-to-one hole, had surrendered at least four goals in every game and had benched goaltender Tim Cheveldae, who donned an electric yellow sports coat in an attempt to change his luck. Plus, Bryan Murray, in his second season, carried an albatross: Despite seven highly successful seasons with Washington, those teams had faltered badly in the playoffs that he had never coached a game in May.

Three games later, the Wings were onto the Norris finals against Chicago — with Game 1 scheduled for May 2 at The Joe. How? The defense tightened. And Cheveldae pitched back-to-back shutouts in Games 5 and 6, including a 1-0 overtime gem on the road, and went 188 minutes and 36 seconds without allowing a goal from the third period of Game 4 to the third period of Game 7.

"When I got a second chance," Cheveldae said, "I told myself, 'Hey, it's just a game, go out and play it. And play it my style.' If they were going to beat me, they were going to beat me in my style of game."

"Isn't that pretty much what the whole team did?" Mitch Albom wrote in the Free Press. "Most of this series, they were dangling over disaster the way Indiana Jones dangles over a pit of snakes. But they always believed they were the better team."

The Wings completed their gut-wrenching comeback with an octopus-filled 5-2 victory at The Joe. (Stars fans had celebrated a Game 3 goal by throwing a walleye on the ice.) The Wings built a 3-0 lead when Sergei Fedorov, Alan Kerr and Gerard Gallant scored during a seven-minute stretch of the opening period. Cheveldae didn't allow a goal until early in the third. Near the end, the 19,875 fans started chanting "Chevy! Chevy! Chevy!" "I sort of enjoyed the moment," he said.

The Wings became the ninth team to overcome a 3-1 deficit in games.

"At no time did we think we couldn't do it," captain Steve Yzerman said. "We're having fun and we want it to continue."

Alas, it did not. The Blackhawks swept the Wings in four tight ones: 2-1, 3-1, 5-4 and 1-0.

First impressions

Only a Red Wing for a few hours, Brendan Shanahan waited a mere three minutes and 31 seconds before engaging in his first fight with his new team. He tangled with Edmonton's Greg de Vries as the opening-night fans in The Joe roared their approved. His teammates were pretty happy to get him, too. "I'm over-excited still," Sergei Fedorov said. "He's real smart," Martin Lapointe said. "He's big, tough, he's got good speed, sees the ice pretty good."

JULIAN H. GONZALEZ/DETROIT FREE PRESS

NO. 34: OCT. 9, 1996

HOCKEYTOWN BECOMES SHANNYTOWN

SHANAHAN'S FIRST DAY: A FLIGHT AND A FIGHT

At the 1996 home opener, the loudest ovations went to the longest-tenured player — Steve Yzerman, a Wing since 1983 — and the newest player — Brendan Shanahan, a Wing since 1 p.m.

The Wings had acquired Shanahan, a tough and talented left wing, from the Hartford Whalers for promising center Keith Primeau, high-scoring defenseman Paul Coffey and a first-round draft choice. He flew from Hartford to Detroit on a jet sent by Mike Ilitch and arrived at The Joe at 6:44 p.m. At the time, fans and likely management regarded Shanahan, twice a 50-goal scorer who averaged 149 penalty minutes a season, as the final piece of the Stanley Cup puzzle.

In his first game, though, Shanahan failed to record a point in a 2-0 victory over Edmonton. But he knew how to thank the fans for their sustained standing ovation: He sought out Greg de Vries for a fight at 3:31 of the first period. His first shift came with Sergei Fedorov at center and Yzerman on the right.

"I see myself as a piece of the puzzle," Shanahan said, "not the only answer. Let's face it, I'm joining an amazing hockey team. One thing they always say about the Red Wings, it's tough to get them off their game. Their game is to win the Stanley Cup, and that's my game, too."

Coach Scotty Bowman didn't temper expectations: "I don't know how many players are like him in the league, a power winger that can score. And obviously, that's what we're expecting."

Shanahan would score 46 goals for the Wings during the regular season and nine more in the playoffs as they did win the Cup. After the home opener, fittingly, the Free Press ran this headline: "Shannytown."

New lease on life

In 1989, nearly three years after his face was sliced open at The Joe, defenseman Borje Salming joined the Red Wings for what would be his final season of a Hall of Fame career. After the incident, Salming said he would wear a shield the rest of his career. "I just called home to Sweden," he told the Toronto Star at the time, "and my mom and my brother told me to wear it from now on. My wife has asked me to wear one for a long time."

WILLIAM DEKAY/DETROIT FREE PRESS

Not half bad

Borje Salming's mug took a lot of abuse over 17 NHL seasons, but Doc Finley kept it from looking far worse. "The cold steel sliced the skin above my right eye, then cut deeply into my nose and along the side of my face," Salming recalled in a 2005 interview for the Hockey Hall of Fame's website.

NO. 35 (TIE): NOV. 26, 1986
A STITCH IN TIME
DOC FINLEY REPAIRS SALMING'S FACE AFTER FRIGHTENING CUT

Toronto defenseman Borje Salming, a future Red Wing and Hockey Hall of Famer, learned what players had said for nearly a half-century in the NHL: If you're going to need stitches, Detroit was the place you wanted to need them.

In the third period, a wild goalmouth scramble ensued in front of Maple Leafs netminder Allan Bester. Bob Probert actually scored on the play (the Wings' lone goal in a 3-1 loss). Salming already was lying on the ice when Wings forward Gerard Gallant was knocked over him. Gallant's skate blade tore into Salming's face, leaving a 5½-inch gash starting above his right eye, just missing the corner of that eye, and ending near the right corner of his mouth.

Doc Finley — John (Jack) Finley, the Wings' team physician for 47 years — rushed into action. He operated late into the night — for 3½ hours at Detroit Osteopathic Hospital

— and used more than 300 stitches to close Salming's wound. He also did plastic surgery on the fly, and reassured Salming that his face would not resemble Frankenstein's monster. As usual, Doc Finely performed his hockey magic. Within months Salming's wounds — considered among the worst injuries in NHL history — were barely visible.

Only days earlier, Salming had discarded a face shield he had donned after an accidental stick broke a bone under his left eye. He complained that the shield impaired his vision.

As the league's oldest player at 38, Salming finished his career with the Wings in 1989-90, compiling a plus-20 rating in 49 games. He then played three more seasons in Sweden, started his own sports underwear line, made the Hall of Fame in 1996 and posed for nude paintings by Swedish graffiti artist Johan A. Wattbert in 2007.

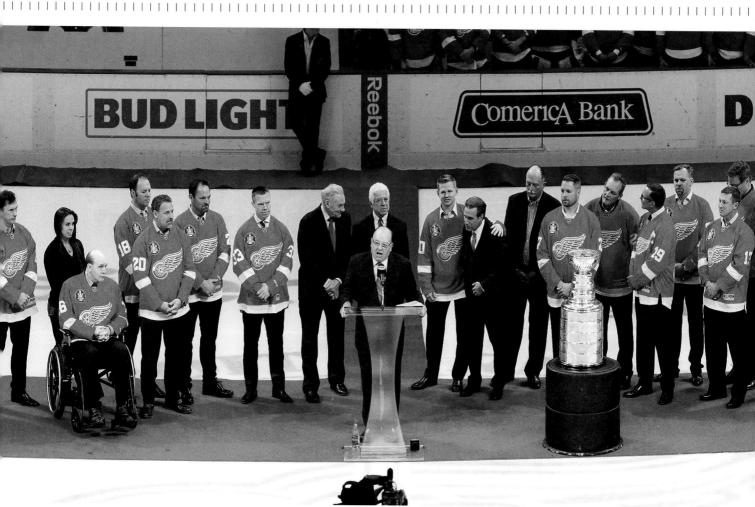

Two decades later

The 1997 Stanley Cup champions basked in the glory again when the Red Wings staged a 20-year reunion as part of the farewell season at Joe Louis Arena. Twenty-one players made it to The Joe — Sergei Fedorov sent a video message — and all were introduced to rousing cheers. The biggest, of course, went to Steve Yzerman. "Finally winning one in '97," Yzerman said at a news conference, "after working through and getting close, it made it pretty special." Only Scotty Bowman spoke to the fans during the ceremony.
RICK OSENTOSKI/USA TODAY SPORTS

NO. 35 (TIE): DEC. 27, 2016

GETTING THE BAND BACK TOGETHER

ON A SPECIAL ANNIVERSARY, THE 1997 CHAMPIONS RETURN TO THE GLORY OF THEIR TIMES

During their farewell season at The Joe, the Red Wings highlighted their long good-bye on an almost nightly basis with special events and guests. Thirty-seven years to the day after their first game in the riverfront arena, the Wings staged a rousing reunion for the 1997 team that ended a 42-year Stanley Cup drought.

Twenty-one of the 25 players donned their old jerseys and basked in the championship glow again, including Vladimir Konstantinov in his wheelchair. They were introduced numerically, from No. 3 Bob Rouse to No. 96 Tomas Holmstrom. Then the coaching staff: assistants Dave Lewis and Barry Smith and their long-time boss, Scotty Bowman. And, lastly, the Stanley Cup itself, carried by Phil Prichard, the famed "Keeper of the Cup." He placed it on a black stand that resembled two giant hockey pucks for all to see and worship.

Bowman spoke to the crowd and called the 1997 champions "a team for the ages." The applause and cheers continued. The players made their exit to a continuous standing ovation, with the Cup held by Darren McCarty.

Before the ceremony, the '97 Wings were given a tour of the Little Caesars Arena construction site, which drew thumbs up but also waves of nostalgia. "You always feel a little bit bad when buildings close," Brendan Shanahan said. "It'll be a beautiful new building."

Shanahan, among 10 Wings who won Cups in '97, '98 and 2002, compared the first and last of those teams: "People would ask me about the 2002 Cup winner, whether that was the best team. I say, 'That might be the most talented team I've been on, but if they play a playoff series against the '97 Wings, they better beat them in four, because the '97 Wings would have beaten them up.' We were younger. We were meaner. ... We were a big, mean, tough team."

NOT SATISFIED WITH HIS PIZZA EMPIRE, HE BROUGHT THE "DEAD WINGS" — AND JOE LOUIS ARENA — BACK TO LIFE, ALL WHILE REMAINING A FRIEND TO THE CITY AND TO HIS PLAYERS

NO EGO FOR MR. I

HE LOVED HIS TEAMS — WIN OR LOSE — JUST AS MUCH AS WE DID

BY MITCH ALBOM

He was always more crust than sauce, a hardworking pizza magnate with a showman's instincts and a shortstop's energy, all tucked beneath a layer of shyness and wonder. No matter how rich he got, Mike Ilitch approached each new challenge like a kid spying a baseball field for the first time. A few years back, when he was 82, I asked him how he viewed his mortality.

"Mortality," he said, a smile cracking his face, "that's a big word."

And the only big thing he couldn't tame.

Say good-bye to Mr. I. No one outskates the clock in this life, and Ilitch's time came to an end on Feb. 10, 2007, at 87, after several years of shaky health. Although his billionaire empire — two major sports teams, a massive food business, theaters, stadiums, entertainment venues and a stream of charities — was enormous, Ilitch himself seemed to wither toward the end, battling health issues, his face gaunter, his suits hanging looser, as if the air were slowly escaping from his joyous balloon.

Still, if anyone defined Rudyard Kipling's famous suggestion to "fill the unforgiving minute with 60 seconds worth of distance run," it was one Michael Ilitch, the son of Macedonian immigrants and the father to a Detroit legacy. It speaks volumes that a man who never hit a ball or stopped a puck professionally was mourned like the biggest sports hero in the city.

Say good-bye to Mr. I. The irony of his nickname is that there was rarely a team owner less about ego. He didn't get into sports to make himself famous, to roam the sidelines or hang in the locker room. Heck, Ilitch didn't even like sitting next to anyone at playoff games, preferring to clench his water bottle alone, his heart racing like the fan he'd always been.

Don't touch it!

Marian and Mike Ilitch posed with Sergei Fedorov after the Wings won the Campbell Bowl as Western Conference playoff champions in 1995. Hockey superstition dictated it's bad luck to handle a trophy before the Stanley Cup.
JULIAN H. GONZALEZ/DETROIT FREE PRESS

Now that seat will forever be empty.

Say good-bye.

NOT LIKE THE OTHERS

Where do you start to describe his influence? You could dive in a lot of places: his business world (a single pizza franchise to a multinational chain), his charity world (from mobile kitchens to youth hockey), his deep investment in Detroit real estate (from

CONTINUED ON PAGE 81

Pair of originals

Red Wings owner Mike Ilitch, standing in front of the original Stanley Cup, showed off his ring as a Hockey Hall of Fame inductee in 2003. He said he couldn't believe the selection committee let a "pizza man in the Hockey Hall of Fame."
KIRTHMON F. DOZIER/DETROIT FREE PRESS

CONTINUED FROM PAGE 80
blocks to buildings, when such investment seemed foolish).

Still, if you spun the dial and it landed on "sports," I'd say you begin not with his four Stanley Cups or two World Series appearances, not with his arenas and stadiums, but with how much he put into building his teams — and how little he put into annoying them. Many owners are caricatures, rich men needing headlines to validate their success. They find the mike. They pound their fists.

Ilitch ruled two franchises with less than half the ego of men who run one.

"Back in the 1990s, there was an owner in hockey that was giving me a hard time," he once told me. "And we were gonna play his team that night. So I go into the locker room and I told the guys,

'If there's ever a game I want you to win it's tonight. ... I want you guys to go out and (teach) him a lesson.'"

The Wings won big. They "skated their asses off," Ilitch recalled. But it wasn't satisfying. He felt sheepish and small.

After that, he said, he changed his attitude. No more locker rooms. No more acting like a coach. His instincts told him "stop." And believe me, getting an owner to stop interfering is a hundred times harder than getting him to start.

CONTINUED ON PAGE 82

CONTINUED FROM PAGE 81

IMPRINT ON THE CITY

About that instinct. It was his North Star, his sailor's compass. Ilitch's face might have been more distinctive, but his gut was his most important feature. He followed it like Dorothy's red shoes, even if the road was, at times, more bumpy stones than yellow brick.

Pizza was not a "smart" investment when he got into it in the late 1950s. But something told him to keep digging deeper. The Red Wings were not a smart investment in 1982, but something told Ilitch there was a treasure under that ice, and his paltry $8-million investment has escalated to a team worth more than $1 billion.

For a while, Mike Ilitch kept the lights on in the city. These days it's vogue to invest in Detroit. Ilitch did it when it was not. There were years when it felt as if Ilitch were lighting candles in a graveyard.

Not anymore. There's Comerica Park. There's Little Caesars' headquarters and Olympia Entertainment. And cranes and heavy equipment surround the rising of Ilitch's final palace, Little Caesars Arena, something he dreamed of years ago, knowing full well, as he told me, "I don't know if I'll see it get built, but it's gonna get done."

There should be something named in his honor at that arena. Because later this year, when they open the doors, there's gonna be an invisible hole smack in the heart of it.

Say good-bye to Mr. I.

ALL FOR HIS PLAYERS

Players. Let's talk about his

CONTINUED ON PAGE 83

Ilitch's All-Stars

Mike Ilitch and Scotty Bowman were front and center when the '02 Wings — with at least nine future Hall of Famers — won the Cup. Mitch Albom wrote in the Free Press: "They came. They clicked. They conquered. There goes the Greatest Hockey Roster Ever Assembled."
JULIAN H. GONZALEZ/DETROIT FREE PRESS

CONTINUED FROM PAGE 82

players. Any rich man can sign star athletes. They smile when you hand them the check and let the door hit you when they split for greener pastures.

Not with Ilitch. When Steve Yzerman, for example, decided to break out on his own, he felt compelled to first visit the Ilitches at their home and explain himself. It was so emotional, Ilitch told me, that his wife, Marian, couldn't come out of a back room because she'd start to cry.

Over the years, so many coaches and players have checked in with Mr. I, both coming and going, you'd have thought he was running Passport Control. But it's a mark of respect, and they all had it for him, just as Ilitch had it for so many of them, never making athletes feel like puppets because he signed their checks.

Don't misunderstand. He could feel slighted. Loyalty mattered to Ilitch only marginally less than it mattered in "The Godfather." The departures of Dave Dombrowski and Prince Fielder carried overtones of Ilitch disappointment. And he once told me that he felt like a fool trying to counsel the oft-troubled Wings Bob Probert and Petr Klima, only to catch them smirking once when he turned his back.

CONTINUED ON PAGE 84

Back-to-back

With Slava Kozlov enjoying their celebration, Mike Ilitch hoisted the 1998 Cup with a little help from his wife, Marian. That made the Wings the first back-to-back champs since 1991-92. Through 2016, there hadn't been another.
JULIAN H. GONZALEZ/DETROIT FREE PRESS

CONTINUED FROM PAGE 83

"I finally woke up and said it takes a heck of a lot more than (me) to keep these guys in line."

TWO SPORTS, ONE OBSESSION

I'll make this observation. Ilitch loved owning a hockey team, but he wasn't crazy about being in baseball. It was too big, too egotistical. He didn't care for some of the other owners, that was my impression, and while he signed some huge contracts he was, as he once told me, "always prepared for a bust."

So why did he do it? Because while hockey became his passion, baseball was his obsession. "I was swinging a bat before I learned my ABC's," he recalled.

And when you have enough money, and your childhood team becomes available ... well, you know how that goes. Ilitch, the onetime Tigers minor-league infielder, has been a good steward of the storied franchise. "That's the thing that hurts so much," Jim Leyland, the former manager, told me. "The fact that we didn't get it for Mike. We knew how bad he wanted it."

ALL FOR THE FANS

For what it's worth, I considered Mr. Ilitch a professional friend. Having known him for 30 years, I think he came to trust me, and I visited his home several times, and we'd sit at a long table and talk about many things, life, family, health. He was incredibly unassuming, often saying "Wow" and shaking his head and looking down.

A true hockey family

Owners Mike and Marian Ilitch gathered their seven children in June 1982 to commemorate the purchase of the Red Wings from Bruce Norris for $8 million.
PATRICIA BECK/ DETROIT FREE PRESS

Yes, he was shrewd. No, he didn't brook dissent. Yes, casino money helped fuel his fortune and, yes, he took advantage of tax breaks.

But nearly every major thing he built, his family still owns. That's the difference between speculating and investing. Mike Ilitch was all portions Detroit. And for a long time, Detroit is going to be a large portion Mike Ilitch.

This was a regular guy who happened to get really rich, a guy who was all about family — one wife, seven kids — who didn't hunger for headlines, didn't collect expensive toys, and never strayed far from his, a man who sometimes felt unwor-

CONTINUED ON PAGE 85

IN THEIR WORDS

Athletes and non-athletes, Detroiters and non-Detroiters alike felt Mike Ilitch's impact. A few of their responses (with some coming via Twitter) on his passing:

PRESIDENT GEORGE W. BUSH (RIGHT): "Mike was a great citizen of our country, a self-made man with talent, drive and a huge heart. My favorite memories with Mike are of our discussions about our shared love, baseball. Another of Mike's passions was his beloved Detroit. He generously gave back to his city and made it a better place."

NHL COMMISSIONER GARY BETTMAN: "Mike's commitment to excellence and winning were unparalleled, and his commitment to the community was unrivaled — as was his boundless support of youth hockey. He was a prolific philanthropist, and, above all, a devoted partner and husband to his wife of 62 years, Marian."

WINGS GM KEN HOLLAND: "To have been able to work with him for more than 30 years and be a part of turning a struggling franchise into a champion again was an experience of a lifetime."

WINGS HALL OF FAMER STEVE YZERMAN: "Both Mr. and Mrs. Ilitch, as well as their entire family, have had an immeasurable impact on not only my career, but my life. Going back to the age of 18 when I arrived in Detroit, the guidance, generosity, concern and love Mr. Ilitch had always shown me and my family are things I will forever be grateful for."

RED WINGS FORWARD JUSTIN ABDELKADER: "Saddened to hear about the passing of Mr. Ilitch. Thanks for all you have done for the city of Detroit and the Red Wings!"

EX-WING MIKE MODANO: "Mr 'I,' thank you for everything you've done."

EX-WING BRENDAN SHANAHAN: "We saw the joyful tears in his eyes when (Steve Yzerman) first handed him the Cup in 1997. We watched him sit bedside Vladimir Konstantinov after his tragic accident a week later. He was more than a team owner. It was personal."

MLB COMMISSIONER ROB MANFRED: "Mike Ilitch was far more than a model owner of the Tigers franchise, the team he loved all his life and played for as a minor leaguer. He was also a fierce believer in his home city of Detroit, and the role that the Tigers and sports played in contributing to civic pride and renewal."

TIGERS GENERAL MANAGER AL AVILA: "I've never seen a man more dedicated to this community and to baseball than Mr. I."

TIGERS PITCHER JUSTIN VERLANDER: "Heartbroken hearing of Mr I's passing. He was a family man. A self-made man. A giving man. An icon for our city and nation."

TIGERS GREAT KIRK GIBSON: "I was just thinking, what's the statue going to look like? Where should it be? He's the guy who created the rebirth of Detroit. It was his vision.... He just wouldn't let barriers get in his way."

DETROIT TIGERS RADIO BROADCASTER DAN DICKERSON: "If you're a fan, what more could you want out of an owner than a guy who was willing to overspend for this market to bring a winning team. ... The other thing you didn't always see was his generosity toward the players, not just in payroll, but the little things he did. I blew out my knee, I had knee surgery while I was working for the team in 2009, and I think he took care of everything that year. I didn't get any bills that year. Those are the kind of things he did, quietly behind the scenes."

PETER KARMANOS, CAROLINA HURRICANES OWNER AND COMPUWARE COFOUNDER: "Though we were rivals on the ice when it came to Little Caesars versus Compuware and the Red Wings against the Hurricanes, I have great respect for what he accomplished as a businessman and owner."

ROGER PENSKE, BIRMINGHAM BUSINESSMAN AND AUTO RACING MOGUL: "From keeping the Red Wings and the Tigers in the downtown area to helping keep the true spirit of Detroit in the forefront, Mike was a real ambassador of our city."

WASHINGTON REDSKINS QB AND EX-SPARTAN KIRK COUSINS: "What a life! Marine, Pro-Athlete, Entrepreneur, Philanthropist. Better believe I'm gonna have a "hot-n-ready" in his honor."

CONTINUED FROM PAGE 84

thy of things but never felt above them.

Perhaps that's why he funded so many huge charity efforts and an equal number of quiet, small ones, like paying Rosa Parks' rent for years, or helping to launch Bright Beginnings, a day care center for infants of mothers going through treatment or homelessness.

More crust than sauce. Mike Ilitch left the spicy stuff to other billionaires. And perhaps because he made his first fortune in pizza, he never forgot that people — especially the customers — mattered.

I asked him once, before he purchased the Tigers, what his priorities would be if he ever got them. He rattled them off, one, two, three. You know what No. 1 was?

The fans.

"I have to please them," he said. "I have to excite them. And I have to earn their respect."

Say good-bye to Mr. I. He died having checked off all three.

THANKS FOR THE MEMORIES

THE NIGHT THE WINGS SHATTERED ROY'S MYSTIQUE

BY NICHOLAS J. COTSONIKA

Joe Louis Arena never went from tension to exhilaration like the night the Red Wings heaped an avalanche on the Avalanche.

May 31, 2002. It was Game 7 of the Western Conference finals between Detroit and Colorado but felt like Game 7 of the Stanley Cup finals, because everyone assumed whichever archrival emerged would beat the waiting Hurricanes.

The Wings had a Hall of Fame coach in Scotty Bowman and nine players who were considered future Hall of Famers at the time: Chris Chelios, Sergei Fedorov, Dominik Hasek, Brett Hull, Igor Larionov, Nicklas Lidstrom, Luc Robitaille, Brendan Shanahan and Steve Yzerman. They had lived up to the hype to that point, dominating the regular season, coming back from a 2-0 deficit to beat the Vancouver Canucks in six games in the first round of the playoffs, beating the St. Louis Blues in five in the second, and coming back from a 3-2 deficit against the Avs to force Game 7.

Now it was all on the line against a team that had beaten them in the playoffs three out of four times since 1996 — against goaltender Patrick Roy, a four-time Cup champion, a three-time playoff MVP. Not only had Roy won his past four Game 7s, he had won his past two by shutout.

The fans showed up early for Hockeytown's most anticipated game in years, some standing outside holding handmade signs to greet the players as they arrived at the rink. Yzerman, the captain, strolled in calmly, as if this were a game against the Nashville Predators on a Monday night in November, coffee cup in his left hand, black leather coat slung over his right shoulder.

As Karen Newman concluded the national anthem, a huge octopus hit the ice. Out came Pete Cusimano, who threw the first octopus in 1952, its eight legs representing the victories needed to win the Cup then, starting a tradition. He picked up this one and held it over his head. The rink roared.

The Wings scored on their first shot, then their second, then their fifth, eighth, 11th, 16th. They scored six goals on their nemesis, and when Roy was pulled 6:28 into the second period and made the lonely skate to the bench, The Joe was jumping, overjoyed. The feeling for the fans and the Wings was a mixture of revenge, relief and disbelief. The Free Press headline would read: "Au Rev-Roy!"

Colorado backup David Aebischer allowed the final goal with 3:51 left, and soon afterward, the fans sang along to Neil Diamond's "Sweet Caroline."

The Wings beat the Avs, 7-0, in the most lopsided Game 7 in NHL history and were off to play Carolina and win the Cup for the third time in six years. Good times never seemed so good.

Nicholas J. Cotsonika covered the Red Wings for the Free Press in 1999-2004 and is now a columnist for NHL.com.

'HA-SEK'S BET-TER! HA-SEK'S BET-TER!'

Maybe Colorado could have stemmed the avalanche of Red Wings goals by putting defenseman Rob Blake in the crease with goaltender Patrick Roy. But on this night, even that likely would not have worked. The sixth goal in Game 7, scored by Fredrik Olausson, sent Roy to the bench at 6:28 of the second period. Nicholas J. Cotsonika wrote for the Free Press: "On a power play, Olausson fired the puck into the upper left corner. "Pa-trick!" … As Roy skated off, his teammates tapped their sticks on his pads, their gloves on his back. Roy took his helmet off, sat down and put a towel around his neck. He smirked, then frowned."

JULIAN H. GONZALEZ/DETROIT FREE PRESS

THE PERSONALITIES, NOT THE BUILDING, ARE WHAT WILL LAST FOREVER FOR ME

BY GEORGE SIPPLE

I covered many great games at Joe Louis Arena, but it's the personalities I watched and interviewed that I remember most.

Once, I was in an elevator with Gordie Howe, the greatest player of all time. He playfully elbowed a young boy, who didn't realize the significance of the act by the gentle giant. The boy's father did, though, and beamed with pride.

The Michigan Wolverines, coached by Red Berenson, won many games at The Joe. A CCHA tourney didn't seem complete unless Berenson uttered one of his familiar "I can't tell you" replies to a query, and then went on to tell you exactly what he thought.

I have great memories of George LaFrance and Ric Flair from when I attended The Joe as a fan. LaFrance was my favorite player on the numerous Detroit Drive teams that won Arena Football League titles. Later, I covered the Detroit Fury, another Arena team, and had several conversations with former Drive coach Tim Marcum about a pro football franchise that brought more titles to the city than the Lions have in my lifetime.

In 1987, I was in the stunned crowd when Flair, a.k.a. Nature Boy, lost the NWA world title to Rugged Ronnie Garvin in a steel cage.

Nicklas Lidstrom and Kris Draper stand out among the Wings I've covered. Lidstrom was the best player I saw play in the Winged Wheel. Sorry, Stevie Y fans. Draper may have been the most accommodating player, always willing to talk to the media. His Grind Line mates were the same way; the latest generation of Wings should emulate this.

I covered an alumni game in which Bob Probert returned to the city and was cheered like the hockey hero he was to many who grew up in the '80s. Sadly, I also was there to cover his funeral in Windsor in 2010.

One of the best personalities at The Joe never played in a game. Al Sobotka maintained the ice, drove the Zamboni and twirled octopi over his head. He also became known for his barbecue meals he made for players.

Of all the Great Lakes Invitationals I covered, the 2012 event was the most memorable. Michigan Tech coach Mel Pearson guided his alma mater to its first GLI title since 1980. Pheonix Copley became the second goaltender in tournament history to post back-to-back shutouts, and he earned MVP honors with 70 saves over two games.

George Sipple has written about every sport under the sun for the Free Press since 1995. These days he spends most of his time covering the Red Wings and Tigers.

Captain Courageous

Two days after a potentially career-threatening knee injury, Steve Yzerman woke up in Madison, Wis., to be prepped for surgery. In the operating room, Dr. William Clancy elected to perform an arthroscopic procedure instead of reconstructive surgery on a severed posterior cruciate ligament. He then issued an optimistic prognosis. Yzerman flew right home and, still groggy, was asleep an hour before the Wings' home game against Minnesota. "If it was on television," he told reporters later at The Joe, "I probably would have stayed home." He arrived late, watched from Mike Ilitch's box and hopped a ride to the locker room to see his teammates. With a 6-3 victory, the first-place Wings clinched a playoff berth with 15 games to go. "Nobody is folding," said coach Jacques Demers. As for his captain? "I knew he would come. I called and told him to stay home."
RICHARD LEE/DETROIT FREE PRESS

ILITCH'S QUICK ACTION AFTER YZERMAN INJURY PAID OFF FOR DECADES

BY KEITH GAVE

On March 1, 1998, general manager Jim Devellano stood with his back to the wall just outside Joe Louis Arena's tiny press room. He looked like someone had just shot his dog.

Moments earlier, Devellano had spoken to the team's medical staff about his star player, Steve Yzerman. The prognosis was alarming and threatened to set the franchise back years, if not decades. After scoring his 50th goal and validating the acclaim that had been building since the Wings drafted him in 1983, Yzerman broke in alone on Buffalo's Tom Barrasso. This time, however, Yzerman lost an edge and slid hard into the unforgiving goalpost to the right of the goalie.

Yzerman, only 22 at the time, lay on the ice, writhing in pain as nearly 20,000 fans began wringing their hands. Devellano was doing the same against that wall, surrounded by reporters.

"He'll need major reconstructive surgery," Devellano said. "The doctors tell me he'll be out for 12-18 months."

Surgery would be performed immediately, Devellano said.

Not so fast, Wings owner Mike Ilitch would say. Before anyone took a knife to his franchise player, Ilitch wanted a second opinion. The next day, he sent Yzerman to Madison, Wis., to see Dr. William Clancy, the country's leading knee specialist who had worked with prominent athletes.

Clancy offered a different opinion: No reconstructive surgery was required. Just a quick arthroscopic procedure. Then build up the muscles around the damaged right knee, and Yzerman should be good to go. Yzerman returned to Detroit and worked feverishly with athletic therapist Jim Pengelly. During his rehabilitation, Yzerman wrote several guest columns for the Free Press. By that, I mean he spoke and I typed on a laptop on my dining room table.

The kid was darn good at that, too. He wrote and read critically: He moved sentences and paragraphs around and built transitions to make it an easier read. But his career as a newspaper columnist was short-lived. In nine weeks — not 18 months, not 12 months, but nine weeks! — Yzerman was back on the ice, playing in the Campbell Conference finals for the second straight year.

An owner's intervention changed everything. And that's just one reason his players loved competing for Ilitch.

A postscript to the story: Starting the next fall, Ilitch made a significant roster change in the medical staff looking after his team.

Keith Gave covered the Red Wings for the Free Press from 1985 through early 1998. In retirement, he is completing a book and helping to write and produce a documentary film about the Russian Five — both of which should be released in 2017.

There was a long, horizontal, green and white highway exit sign that I always loved spotting in the concourse area of The Joe near the team locker rooms:

BY STEVE KORNACKI

Olympia Stadium
EXIT WARREN AVE

The sign was a connection to our original hockey palace at our second hockey home. The sign always made me think about the foundation of a great franchise, where the Winged Wheel was first worn and the original and second-coming Production Lines skated, with Gordie Howe the star of both.

I remember talking to Steve Yzerman about the birth of his first daughter near that Olympia sign after a morning skate. Even describing his biggest goals didn't elicit that much joy.

Another day, just down the hallway from there, I awaited Sergei Fedorov for an interview. He was in the middle of his Hart Trophy MVP season in 1993-94, and he agreed that morning to meet me at a specific time before the game. That time came and passed, and just before the locker room was about to close to reporters, Fedorov arrived, hurried and apologetic.

"Come with me," he said, waving me into the locker room.

He needed to go straight to the trainer's room to get taped and prepared for the game, and motioned me in there, too. When I explained that reporters weren't allowed there, he smiled and

shook his head.

"You can come in here with me," Fedorov said. "I will make it OK."

I had that uneasy feeling you get when you are told that something you know is wrong really isn't, but I was up for the adventure. We had a pleasant conversation as he sat on the table getting tended to, and I stood by his side, writing his quotes in my notebook. Just as he finished answering my final question, a member of the media relations staff burst in and shouted, "WHAT are you doing in here?"

I explained it was Sergei's idea and Sergei smiled and nodded, assuring him that it was OK. But I knew it was time to exit. I had my story. Sergei winked and nodded as I departed.

Later that season, I was the only Freep staffer to pick the eighth-seeded Sharks to take the first-round series from the Wings. Family members disowned me, and fans at The Joe before Game 7 recognized me walking to my press seat, which was just above the top row of that spectator section. They said some mean things, but I did my best to ignore them. My editors frowned upon getting into brawls with our readers, no matter how

uncouth some of them were.

The Sharks won that game, 3-2, and took the series in a huge upset. I didn't hear another word as I worked my way down press row to the elevator, but I still felt badly. The Wings' Cup quest would last three more years, and by then I'd be writing for the Orlando Sentinel and watching on TV as The Joe exploded in joy after the sweep of the Flyers.

The Joe has meant so much to so many people. Michigan hockey coach Red Berenson, whose fantastic NHL playing career ended the year before it opened, has shared how special the place is because of the Great Lakes Invitational and conference tournaments his Wolverines played there, and the feeling he gets from coaching the game before fans who know it.

I'm hoping that Olympia exit sign makes its way to the new arena just off I-75, and that something from The Joe finds its way there, too.

Steve Kornacki, a Free Press sports writer in 1988-97, writes for the Michigan athletic website, mgoblue. com. He grew up in the hockey hotbed of Trenton, Mich., but somehow never mastered skating. However, he dreams of driving a Zamboni someday and twirling an octopus from it.

WORKING AT THE JOE MEANT NAVIGATING SOME TIGHT SQUEEZES

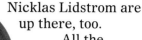

BY HELENE ST. JAMES

Famously, the press box at Joe Louis Arena was an afterthought, forgotten in the original planning stages. That made for an interesting workplace.

There isn't a more intimate press box in the NHL. Some press boxes, such as Minnesota's XCel Energy Center, could host a ballet they were so roomy. At The Joe, people have to walk single file. Three people standing around talking to one another creates a traffic jam. My seat is next to a pillar, which means 90% of the people who pass by bump into me. Some, in an effort to make more room, just tip the chair forward, with me in it.

It's a great view, though, because we sit much closer to the ice than at most other places. Essentially, we are in the last row of the upper bowl, and The Joe's atmosphere is much closer than in places where we sit near the rafters.

One of the first games I covered at The Joe was Sergei Fedorov's five-goal night, Dec. 26, 1996. That started what has become a slew of amazing memories. The June 7, 1997, end to the 42-year Stanley Cup drought is another highlight. The 7-0 playoff game against Colorado in 2002. The retirement ceremonies for Steve Yzerman and

Nicklas Lidstrom are up there, too.

All the players through the years — Slava Fetisov was a bona fide hockey legend when he joined the Wings in 1995, and couldn't have been kinder and more accessible. Yzerman spoke softly, but what a sense of humor he has. Lidstrom remains the politest person I have ever encountered. Tomas Holmstrom is one of the funniest — his January 2013 retirement news conference in the Olympia room had the audience chuckling nonstop.

Some former players are now Wings personnel, so I often see Kirk Maltby, Kris Draper, Chris Chelios and Jiri Fischer in the press box, all highly entertaining.

After leaving The Joe following a game, I still usually depart with a laugh. The shortest distance to the press parking area involves climbing between a fence and a pillar. In winter, this often means forging through snow and ice. Shimmying along the pillar and jumping back down, my colleagues and I joke about the glamour of it all. The Joe might be lacking in some areas, but it's never been a boring place to work.

Helene St. James has covered the Red Wings since joining the Free Press in 1995 and has been the main beat reporter since 2005.

Survival of the fittest

After a hard night at the office — in her case, the press box at Joe Louis Arena — Free Press beat writer Helene St. James' work wasn't over until she squeezed between a concrete pillar and a chain-link fence to reach the press parking area. The winter chill off the Detroit River, ice and snow only added to the physical challenge.

REMEMBERING THE NIGHT I KEPT A DETROIT TRADITION ALIVE

BY BERNIE CZARNIECKI

As a huge fan of Olympia Stadium, I was depressed initially by the Red Wings' move to Joe Louis Arena in December 1979.

Gordie Howe returning to Detroit ice three times in 1980 eased my pain. Howe played two thrilling games for the Hartford Whalers and one mind-blowing appearance for the Prince of Wales Conference in the 32nd All-Star Game — all to packed houses and numerous emotional standing ovations.

But the thrill of thrills was fulfilling a lifelong fantasy of throwing an octopus on Detroit ice! It happened March 26, 1985, against the Minnesota North Stars.

The Wings had clinched the playoffs a few games earlier, but no one had thrown an octopus because the team had threatened to have any octopus throwers arrested after a fan was hit by one during the 1984 playoffs.

The threat frustrated me, but I was determined to keep a Detroit tradition alive, one that had started April 15, 1952, by brothers Pete and Jerry Cusimano during the Stanley Cup playoffs. So, with longtime buddy Steve Dluzynski as my wingman, I went to the Fish Market on Schaefer Road in Dearborn and picked out a hefty five-pounder to be hurled on the ice that night.

I smuggled the octopus into The Joe in a tattered camera case I bought at a garage sale. After settling in with several friends in the upper bowl, I sat with beer in hand and octopus under my seat and waited for just the right moment, which I had decided would be John Ogrodnick's 53rd goal, which would break Mickey Redmond's team record.

I sat through the first two periods with Mr. Octopi under my seat, but, alas, no Ogrodnick goal occurred.

The octopus was beginning to take its toll on the olfactory system. So much so that, during the second period, I had to take the octopus into the bathroom to rinse it off because the stench was starting to overwhelm the upper-bowl neighborhood.

Just as I was giving it a sink bath, a Detroit policeman walked in

CONTINUED ON PAGE 94

Occupational hazard

Every sports town has its traditions, but few must be odder than Detroit's penchant for throwing an octopus at a hockey game. Pete Cusimano threw the first one at Olympia during the 1952 playoffs. Its eight tentacles were to represent the victories needed to win the Stanley Cup. Over the decades, the unwritten rules of when to throw an octopus were loosened. These days, you throw 'em if you got 'em. If it's a big game or a milestone moment or a playoff victory all the better. In March 2016, as the Wings were struggling to extend their playoff streak to 25 straight seasons, an octopus landed during the third period against Buffalo. Maria Rotondo of the ice crew answered the call of duty.

KIMBERLY P. MITCHELL/DETROIT FREE PRESS

CONTINUED FROM PAGE 92

and freaked me out. I envisioned myself being handcuffed and escorted out of the bathroom holding an octopus. I quickly shoved it back into its plastic bag, and then into the camera case, and hurried back to my seat.

By the end of the second period, I was getting more and more worried that Ogrodnick was not going to score. I went to the concourse with my older brother Tom, who bought me a shot of Canadian Club for good luck.

The third period already had started as we headed back to our seats. But the moment we reached the standing-room area between the upper and lower bowls, Ogrodnick got the puck on his stick and scored goal No. 53 right in front of us.

Adrenaline and elation immediately took over.

I had no time to waste. I knelt down near the SRO wall, grabbed the octopus from the camera case and raced down the lower-bowl steps behind the goal with the stenchy five-pounder in the palm of my right hand; its long tentacles dangled over and through my fingers like slimy dreadlocks.

I stopped about 10 rows from the bottom and shot-putted the octopus over the glass. It cleared with room to spare, landed at the rim of the circle to the right of the North Stars' goal, slid about 10 feet and stopped right on the face-off dot, its eight tentacles fully extended — as perfect a landing as I ever could had hoped for.

The crowd, already giving Ogrodnick a standing ovation, ripped into an absolute frenzy when the octopus hit the ice. Beaming, I headed up the steps, laughing and high-fiving everyone on both sides of the aisle with my still-slimy right hand. Everyone was so pumped that nobody seemed to mind.

Near the top, I saw my brother, beer in hand, his smiling face as red as the goal light, yelling over and over, "I CAN'T BELIEVE YOU DID IT! I CAN'T BELIEVE YOU DID IT!"

When I reached the top, I noticed a policeman standing behind my brother. Again, I feared that I was going to be arrested. But the officer stood stone-faced with his hands by his side.

Back at my seat in the upper bowl, my supercharged friends mobbed me. The Wings won, 5-1, and all was right with the hockey world.

When I got home, I listened to a recording of Ogrodnick's goal from the broadcast on WJR-AM (760). Hall of Famer Sid Abel, the analyst for Bruce Martyn at the time, was describing the "standing ovation of John Ogrodnick" when his voice rose to another level as he exclaimed "and there's the first octopus of the season being thrown on the ice! ... And it's a BIG ONE!"

I swelled with pride, having my act of Red Wings love described so enthusiastically by Old Bootnose. And as a die-hard Wings fan, I believed that I could die and my hockey life would have been fulfilled.

No charges were leveled against me — or anyone else — for throwing an octopus. And the rest is joyful Red Wings history.

Bernie Czarniecki, who grew up on Detroit's west side, worked as an agate editor at the Free Press in 1980-2009.

20,000 leagues under The Joe
Red Wings fans Abbie Genautis and Michael Johnson of Troy risked their lives against the giant tentacles of Al the Octopus. The Wings painted the steep entrance steps before their 2015 playoff series against Tampa Bay.
DIANE WEISS/DETROIT FREE PRESS

IN THE BEGINNING, THE JOE WAS BEST KNOWN FOR WHAT WAS MISSING

BY BILL MCGRAW

Joe Louis Arena was missing a few things when the Red Wings began playing in the $34-million arena on the riverfront.

On Dec 27, 1979:

There was no advertising, no executive suites, no parking garage, no photos or banners or any of the multiple decorative flourishes that later filled the arena.

There was no National Hockey League team.

OK, the Red Wings technically belonged to the NHL, although the Red Wings of 38 years ago were the "Dead Things" who remained stuck in their long "Darkness with Harkness" era. In their first game at The Joe, the Wings fittingly blew a lead and lost to the Blues, 3-2.

The city-owned arena looked bare when play began. There wasn't even a press box until the last minute, when it suddenly dawned on construction officials that they needed to set aside a little space for the media.

In the beginning, arena officials couldn't get the ice right: It was too soft, and players complained that it made them slow. For most Wings, that was merely an excuse.

In the restrooms, they didn't install enough urinals, so many male fans used the sinks instead. Yes, male fans stood in line to urinate in the sinks. The lines for the women's restrooms were endless.

Without any adornments, the arena looked more immense than it does today. It seemed naked and vast, and fans complained it lacked Olympia's coziness and they couldn't hear the pucks banging off the boards and the players' skates on the ice.

On the plus side, they began selling beer in bigger quantities at The Joe, and it cost only $2.25. Tickets were $11, $10, $9 and $7.

And all 19,742 fans at the opening hockey game received signed certificates from two strange bedfellows, team general manager Ted Lindsay and Detroit Mayor Coleman Young.

Bill McGraw, a 2014 inductee to the Michigan Journalism Hall of Fame, covered the Red Wings in 1979-83 during his 37 years with the Free Press.

THE "WAREHOUSE ON THE WATER" HAS PROVOKED A LOT OF STRONG EMOTIONS OVER THE YEARS FROM THE FOLKS WHO SPENT THE MOST TIME THERE. LONGTIME EMPLOYEES ...

SOUND OFF

FROM INTERVIEWS BY BILL DOW

AL SOBOTKA, BUILDING OPERATIONS MANAGER: "I've worked with the Wings since 1971, so when we moved from Olympia Stadium to Joe Louis Arena, it was like night and day, just as it will be when we move into the new arena. The arena was state of the art in 1980, and overall it's been a great building, especially after the Ilitches upgraded it."

JOHN OGRODNICK, RED WINGS SNIPER, 1979-87: "I started my career in Detroit soon after it opened. Unlike Olympia Stadium, there just was no history in the building. Normally practices are at 10 or 11 a.m., but when I got called up, we used to practice at 2 or 3 in the afternoon because we had to let the construction workers continue to finish the building and there was still a lot of work to do. That was interesting."

DARREN MCCARTY, GRIND LINER FOR FOUR RED WINGS STANLEY CUPS: "My relationship with the arena dates back to my youth growing up in Leamington (Ontario). I lived through the Dead Wings era, and at that time the Ilitches were giving away a car a game to get fans in the seats. We would sit in the upper bowl, but then halfway through the first period, we would go down and sit along the glass because no one would be there."

STEVE YZERMAN, HALL OF FAME RED WING: "It's been a fantastic building. It's a great building to play in. If you watch games as fans, the atmosphere is fantastic."

MARK HOWE, GORDIE'S SON, RED WINGS EXECUTIVE AND FORMER WING: "My fondest memory was as an opponent when I played for the Hartford Whalers with my dad and my brother Marty the year Joe Louis Arena opened. Our coach, Don Blackburn, knew it was special that we were back in Detroit, so he started the game with my dad at center, I was at right wing and Marty was the left winger. This was the only time we would ever play on a line together. We had been on the ice at the same time before, but Marty was a defenseman and at that time I was a forward. Blackburn

No barbecued octopus?

Building operations manager Al Sobotka, also the Zamboni driver and octopus twirler, fired up the grill outside The Joe for his annual playoff barbecue for the Red Wings' players and staff. On the menu for the 2008 playoff run — which would end with Detroit's 11th Stanley Cup — were ribs, chicken, burgers and sausage.
WILLIAM ARCHIE/DETROIT FREE PRESS

told us that as soon as the puck dropped Marty was to go to the bench. His replacement already had one leg over the board. My dad told us to ignore it and that we were going to play the whole shift. Dad just wanted to enjoy the moment."

SOBOTKA AGAIN: "For nearly 20 years now, we have had fans and celebrities ride the Zamboni in between periods, and it's been great seeing how much they enjoy it. I have driven Kwame Kil-

patrick, Ndamukong Suh and other well-known people. One time during a practice, Gordie Howe drove with me, and he got the biggest kick out of it. He said, 'After all these years, look at me.'"

GORDIE HOWE, AFTER HIS FIRST GAME AT THE JOE IN 1980: "The people make the rink."

MCCARTY AGAIN: "When I was 12, my peewee team played there, but because of some crazy league rule,

CONTINUED ON PAGE 98

A Lion named Suh

During the 2013 Stanley Cup playoffs, Lions All-Pro defensive tackle Ndamukong Suh became the latest celebrity to go for a ride on the Zamboni. Driver Al Sobotka never ceased to be amazed at how much celebrities enjoyed their laps resurfacing the ice between periods. "Recently," he said, "I had Michael Fulmer, the Tigers' pitcher who was last year's American League rookie of the year. He absolutely loved it and thanked me for a great experience." After the 2014 season, Suh bolted from the Lions for the Miami Dolphins, signing a six-year, $114-million contract that included a whopping $60 million guaranteed.

KIRTHMON F. DOZIER/DETROIT FREE PRESS

CONTINUED FROM PAGE 96

they wouldn't let me. That pissed me off losing a chance to skate on an NHL rink, and I vowed that I would play there one day."

SCOTTY BOWMAN: RED WINGS COACH, 1993-2002: "We had a lot of success there, but when I think of Joe Louis Arena, what first comes to mind are the people at the rink. We knew all the employees by their first name. I don't think you could ever re-create the friendly atmosphere of the place. It was also so easy to get around. You parked right next to it, headed to the locker room, and the offices were right close by."

ELLIOTT TRUMBULL, RED WINGS PR DIRECTOR, 1958-65: "My favorite memory of the arena was being present in the building when we won the Cup in 1997. Mike Ilitch contacted Gary Bergman, president of the Red Wings Alumni Association, and invited the alumni to be in the arena for Game 4. Tickets were not available, so we gathered in the alumni room in the basement of the arena and watched it on TV. I couldn't stand the suspense, so in the closing minutes I went upstairs and an usher let me stand to watch the end of the game and postgame ceremonies. I went back to the alumni room, and Gary had gone into the Wings' dressing room and brought back some champagne so we could all celebrate. The building was still shaking with all the noise. I remem-

ber walking out of the arena with Budd Lynch about 3 a.m. on that wonderful June morning. I have to thank Mike Ilitch, because he always thinks of the former players and is cognizant of Red Wing history."

‹‹ MCCARTY AGAIN: "A good fight was part of our strategy because it fired up the crowd and the team. My favorite thing was, after I fought, skating off the ice and just listening to the crowd going nuts."

BOWMAN AGAIN: "The building had a lot of atmosphere and it was very noisy, especially in the playoffs when the crowd got going. It was an advantage for us to play there with those great fans."

SOBOTKA AGAIN: "When we won the Cup in '97, I went onto the ice and Sergei Federov handed me the Cup. When I carried it over my head, some of the players teased me, but I said, 'I have a lot more seniority than you do.'"

‹‹ MARK HOWE AGAIN: "In my second year as a scout for the Wings, I was at the game when we won the Stanley Cup for the first time in 42 years. I felt a part of the Red Wings growing up as a kid. It was frustrating that in the '60s we lost in the finals four times before the team became bad for so many years. When Darren McCarty scored that great goal against my old team-

CONTINUED ON PAGE 99

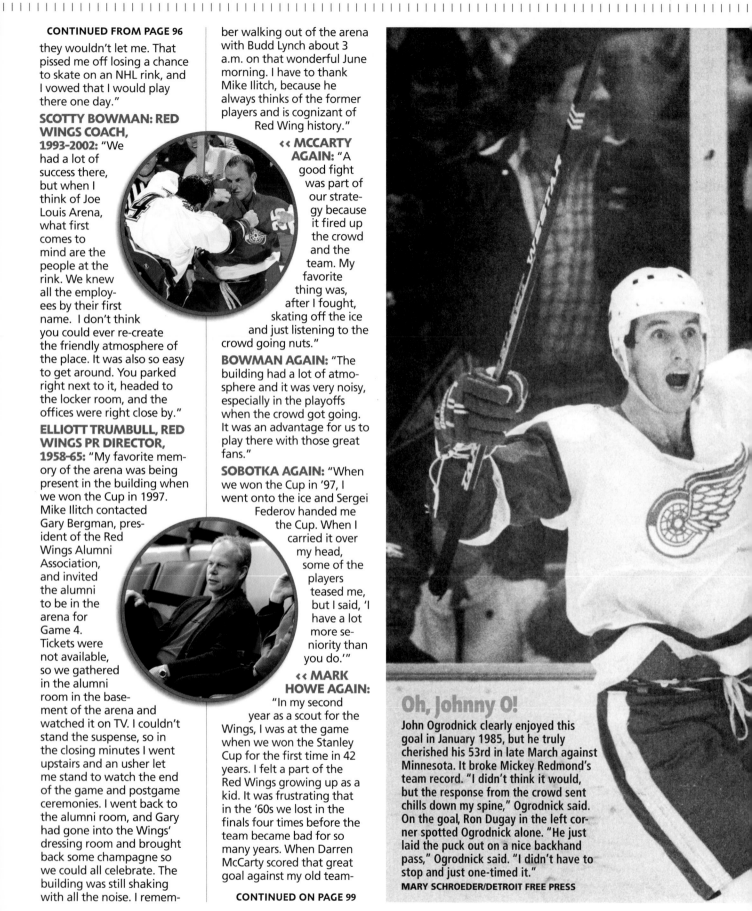

Oh, Johnny O!

John Ogrodnick clearly enjoyed this goal in January 1985, but he truly cherished his 53rd in late March against Minnesota. It broke Mickey Redmond's team record. "I didn't think it would, but the response from the crowd sent chills down my spine," Ogrodnick said. On the goal, Ron Dugay in the left corner spotted Ogrodnick alone. "He just laid the puck out on a nice backhand pass," Ogrodnick said. "I didn't have to stop and just one-timed it."

MARY SCHROEDER/DETROIT FREE PRESS

That's Fats!

The Red Wings honored two-thirds of the second Production Line on consecutive home dates in October 2008. They unveiled a statue of center Alex Delvecchio on Thursday night and another for left wing Ted Lindsay on Saturday night. A statue of their right wing, Gordie Howe, had been unveiled the previous year. All three were sculpted by noted artist Omri Amrany. Delvecchio spent his entire 23-year career with the Wings, the last 12 as captain. Only Steve Yzerman's captaincy was longer in Detroit. Later, Delvecchio served as Wings coach, general manager and broadcaster. All three statues were expected to move with the team to the new Little Caesars Arena in 2017. "I'm looking forward to seeing the new place," Delvecchio told nhl.com a year before its expected opening. "I just hope I'm still around to see it."

JULIAN H. GONZALEZ/
DETROIT FREE PRESS

CONTINUED FROM PAGE 98

mate Hexie (Ron Hextall), the building just exploded. When the game ended, security wouldn't let me on the ice because they said there were too many on it. Thankfully, John Hahn, our media relations director, convinced them to let me go on the ice. I have a great photo taken in locker room afterwards with my youngest son, Nolan, the Cup, Vladdie (Konstantinov) and Nick (Lidstrom)."

‹‹ OGRODNICK AGAIN: "I'll never forget when the crowd gave me a wonderful standing ovation at the arena when I scored my 53rd goal of the '84-85 season to pass Mickey Redmond for the team record. That was special. I was surprised and very disappointed when I was traded because I enjoyed playing for the Wings."

JIM HAWKINS, FREE PRESS COLUMNIST IN 1981: "Heavyweight championship boxing returned to the Motor City for the first time in 11 years. If we are re- ally lucky, it won't come back again until 1992. By then, maybe, somebody will have formally dedicated the ugly warehouse on the water that bears Joe Louis' name."

SOBOTKA AGAIN: "People don't realize how hard it is to operate the place, especially when other special events take place just before a hockey game. There can be a lot of long hours. That being said, I have truly enjoyed it."

AIN'T NO PARTY LIKE A JOE LOUIS ARENA PARTY, RIGHT? OK, IT DIDN'T GET OFF TO A ROUSING START IN 1979 AND IT'S SLOWED DOWN IN RECENT YEARS, BUT IT ROCKED IN THE '90S AND ON, DIDN'T IT? SO LET'S REMEMBER SOME OF THE GOOD TIMES THAT ACCOMPANIED THE GREAT HOCKEY, HERE IN THE ...

OCTOPUS GARDEN

BY STEVE SCHRADER

'POD CAST

That's as in cephalopod, because The Joe is where so many octopi went to fly. And then swim, as they apparently were disposed of in the Detroit River after being cast on the ice.

The tradition actually started at the Olympia in the spring of 1952 when brothers Pete and Jerry Cusimano, who owned a fish market, threw an octopus on the ice because, they said, its eight tentacles represented the eight playoff victories needed to win the Stanley Cup. And the Wings did that year, going a perfect 8-0.

Symbolically, it didn't work after expansion, and the Wings weren't a Cup threat for a few decades anyway. But they were in the '90s, and the tradition was revived, too, with scores of octopi hitting the ice at The Joe. Once obscure, now hockey fans couldn't think Detroit without thinking octopus.

One clip in the "Coach's Corner" opening on CBC's "Hockey Night in Canada" even showed Don Cherry as a typical Wings fan, wearing sunglasses, a backward ballcap, black sleeveless T-shirt and hoisting a big, slimy octopus overhead.

Capitals' punishment

After octopi flew, they often received an escort off the ice and a twirl overhead from Al Sobotka, the building operations manager at The Joe. This 'pi landed during a first-period break in Game 1 of the 1998 Stanley Cup finals. By defeating the Washington Capitals in five games, the Red Wings became the first team to win back-to-back Cups since Pittsburgh in 1991-92. Entering the 2017 playoffs, no team had won back-to-back Cups since.

KIRTHMON F. DOZIER/DETROIT FREE PRESS

THE LIFE OF 'PI

Here's a little more of what we remember from the era:

WHO WANTS 'PI? If it's not available at your local seafood market, Superior Fish in Royal Oak dubbed itself the "O-Fish-AL" octopi supply store and published its rules of "Octoquette," which included tips like boiling the 'pi first, throwing them only after Wings goals and aiming for open ice.

HERE'S ONE MORE: Make sure you're close enough, because some fans overestimated their arm strength and couldn't get them over the glass.

SNEAKING THEM IN: Octopi might be a beloved tradition for Wings fans, but it's much more cherished as a marketing tool for the team. So, octopi are among the banned items at The Joe.

Of course, the metal detectors will be no problem, but beware the security guard who asked, "Is that an octopus in your pocket or are you just glad to see the Wings?" Concealing octopi — hopefully sealed in a leakproof plastic bag — in one's trousers was a preferred method of smuggling them into The Joe.

WHAT'S YOUR NAME? The Freep referred to that large and hairless octopus character the Wings came up with for a logo as "Homer," because it resembles a certain Simpson (and not Tomas Holmstrom). But the Wings named it Al, after Zamboni driver Al Sobotka, who was in charge of removing the octopi from the ice.

SPECIAL FEATURES

Some of the physical features we'll remember from The Joe:

THE BANNERS: The numerous red-and-white banners hanging from the ceiling ranged from those for the Wings' 11 Stanley Cups (four of them from The Joe years) and seven retired jerseys (not counting Larry Aurie's No. 6) all the way down to things like Norris Division playoff champions.

THE MEN'S ROOM: It featured multipurpose sinks that some guys even used to wash their hands.

THE LADIES ROOM: It featured long, long lines, maybe even longer than the line of Wings goalies that paraded through The Joe.

(And if you thought the ladies' lines were long for hockey games, you should have seen figure skating events held there. And no waiting for the men's.)

THE SCORE-O BOARD: Some nights it stopped more pucks than Wings goalies. Is that another goalie joke?

THE PRESS BOX: It was just an afterthought when The Joe was built, the story goes, basically a long, cramped space with barely enough room to squeeze through once the media were seated. Donald Trump would approve.

The Real Fab Five

The Russian Five famously posed for posterity after a practice at Joe Louis Arena in 1996. From the left: Slava Fetisov, Sergei Fedorov, Vladimir Konstantinov, Igor Larionov and Slava Kozlov.

J. KYLE KEENER/DETROIT FREE PRESS

ALSO KNOWN AS ...

Speaking of nicknames, and since the title of this book is a nickname, here are some more from the era (not counting typical hockey nicknames like Drapes, Malts, Ozzie, Shanny, Kronner and Cheli):

AREN'T YOU SPECIAL: Mr. Hockey (Gordie Howe, who did play at The Joe, but as a Hartford Whaler in 1980), The Perfect Human (Nicklas Lidstrom), The Magic Man (Pavel Datsyuk), The Professor (Igor Larionov).

GROUPS: The Bruise Brothers (Joe Kocur and Bob Probert), the Grind Line (Kris Draper, Kirk Maltby and Kocur/Darren McCarty), the Russian Five (Slava Fetisov, Vladimir Konstantinov, Larionov, Sergei Fedorov and Slava Kozlov), the Swedish Five (Lidstrom, Niklas Kronwall, Henrik Zetterberg, Mikael Samuelsson and Tomas Holmstrom).

DISPARAGING NICKNAMES: Fats (Alex Delvecchio, who didn't play there but does have a statue at The Joe), the Dead Wings (the effects of Darkness with Harkness at the Olympia).

LETTERMEN: Stevie Y (Steve Yzerman, a.k.a. the Captain), Johnny O (John Ogrodnick), the Little M (Peter Mahovlich), Mr. I (Mike Ilitch), Z (Zetterberg).

NICKNAMES DESIGNED TO MAKE YOU THINK, "MAYBE I BETTER NOT MESS WITH THIS GUY": Vlad the Impaler (Konstantinov), Demolition Man (Holmstrom, a.k.a. Homer), Little Ball of Hate (Pat Verbeek), Probie.

OUR TOWN: The Red Wings renamed it Hockeytown, which is cool. On "Hockey Night in Canada" it's called dee-TROY-it, which is cooler.

OTHER WILD LIFE

Besides octopi, the Joe's fauna boasted:

THE MULE: Although Johan Franzen sightings became rather rare.

THE GOOSE: Maybe a change of scenery will do Gustav Nyquist some good.

TWO KIDS AND AN OLD GOAT: The ageist nickname for the line of Pavel Datsyuk, Boyd Devereaux and Brett Hull from the 2002 championship team.

THE TURTLE: Remember Claude Lemieux whining, "Why me, why me?" Or was that someone else?

STAR POWER

A few of the celebrities you might have seen at The Joe:

ANNA KOURNIKOVA: The Wings had many lovely significant others over the years, but Sergei Fedorov's teen angel was The Joe's top WAG.

JEFF DANIELS: The Emmy-winning actor from Chelsea is a devoted fan of all Detroit sports.

TIM ALLEN: The Birmingham funnyman wore Wings (and many other Detroit sports) T-shirts and jerseys as Tim Taylor on "Home Improvement" (not to be confused with the Tim Taylor who played himself on the Wings).

DAVE COULIER: Uncle Joey from "Full House" even coached the Centennial Classic Wings Alumni at Toronto.

HARRY POTTER: What? Yes, British actor Daniel Radcliffe magically has appeared at The Joe with his girlfriend, actress/Wings fan Erin Darke of Flint.

JOHN CUSACK: That seems even more unlikely, being from Chicago, but he hung around The Joe because of buddy Chris Chelios.

KRISTEN BELL AND DAX SHEPARD: The Hollywood couple hail from Huntington Woods and Milford, respectively, but one of their first meetings was at a Wings game — in L.A. And her show "The Good Place" apparently is not about The Joe.

STEVEN YEUN: The actor from Troy played Glenn on "The Walking Dead" before he was high-sticked by Negan.

VILLAINS

The Joe has had its share of Red Wings heroes, but it wouldn't be nearly as much fun without some very special villains, too. Here are a few that Detroit fans loved to boo:

CLAUDE LEMIEUX: He was the worst, when he punctuated the Red Wings' disappointing loss in the 1996 Western Conference finals by sending Kris Draper facefirst into the boards at Denver and launching that era's rivalry with the Colorado Avalanche. And then a hero was born the next season when Darren McCarty pummeled a turtling Lemieux in the regular-season rematch at The Joe.

MARC CRAWFORD: The head of the Avs' asylum back in the day was their coach, typified by a tantrum he threw in a '97 conference finals loss at Detroit, when he got in Scotty Bowman's face and screamed about the metal plate in his head.

JOHN BROPHY: Before there was Crawford, there was Brophy. His Toronto Maple Leafs battled the Wings in the down-and-dirty Norris Division, and he taunted Jacques Demers.

NATIONAL NETWORK ANNOUNCERS: For those of you watching at home on TV, they always were against the Wings.

KERRY FRASER: Don't you still just want to muss up this referee's hair?

TONYA HARDING AND HER CREW: The attack on rival figure skater Nancy Kerrigan actually happened at Cobo, but close enough.

GARY BETTMAN: The Commish never failed to get booed at The Joe, even when he came bearing the Stanley Cup.

PATRICK ROY: He ticked off fans with his mouth and lousy attitude for the dreaded Avs. He also was known for getting in the way of shots from Wings shooters' sticks and goalies' fists. But one shot St. Patrick didn't stop at The Joe was Steve Yzerman's 500th goal.

There also were a few villains who saw the error of their ways and came around to the Red Wings' side, like Chris Chelios, Dino Ciccarelli and Todd Bertuzzi. Sergei Fedorov turned into a villain when he left as a free agent, but over the years all was forgiven.

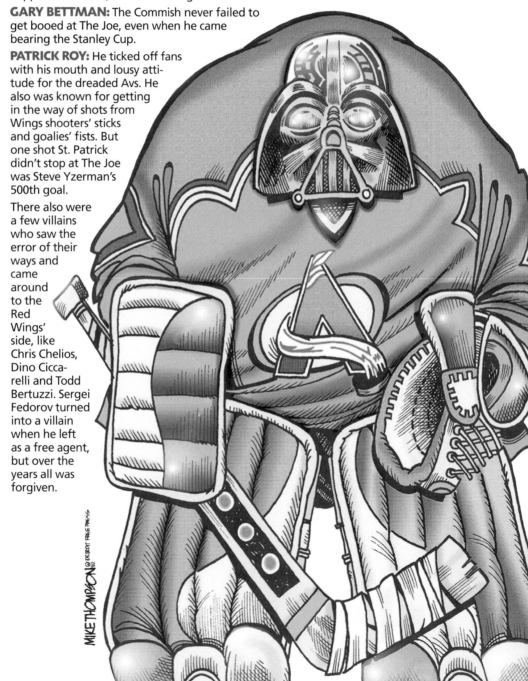

MIKE THOMPSON @ DETROIT FREE PRESS

The flying songstress

Al the Octopus was being held prisoner, and only Karen could save him! That was the premise of the pregame video production for the playoffs, which set up a grand real-life entrance by Red Wings anthem singer Karen Newman. She swooped down like an avenging angel, lowered from high above The Joe's ice by cables — just like Al.
KIRTHMON F. DOZIER/DETROIT FREE PRESS

SOUNDTRACK

Besides Karen Newman, here were some of the Red Wings' sounds of the era (and some you can find on YouTube):

ORIGINAL SONGS: It started in '96 with "I Want Stanley," a catchy theme sung to the tune of "I Want Candy." Well, you can't always get what you want, because the Wings didn't win the Cup that year. But the tradition of playoff theme songs continued with more forgettable tunes like "Get Up!," "Are You Ready, Hockeytown," "Get Your Red On" and "Let 'Em See Red." But one song that has survived is "Hey, Hey, Hockeytown."

FAN MUSIC: The best is 2002's "Without Stanley," rapped to Eminem's "Without Me."

‹‹ LET'S GET A BAND TOGETHER: Darren McCarty rode his hockey fame to fulfilling another dream: Playing in a rock band, Grinder, named for his Wings line.

SUPPORTING CAST

The players were the stars, of course, but they weren't the only personalities at The Joe:

KAREN NEWMAN: The Red Wings' Own always got games started with an air of anticipation for fans at The Joe: "What's Karen wearing tonight?" She began singing "The Star-Spangled Banner" and "O Canada" more than a quarter-century ago, starting, she says, on the same day as Sergei Fedorov. And during the 1998 playoffs, she also was known for being lowered to the ice from the rafters, and then dashing off the ice to make a daring quick-change from her black catsuit to a red, sequined dress before singing.

AL SOBOTKA: The aforementioned Sobotka became a familiar figure from the way he fetched the thrown octopi from the ice. While others — especially at away games — wouldn't even touch the slimy creatures, Sobotka twirled them over his head. Detroit fans loved his act, but of course the league didn't and banned it (especially since the tradition had begun to spread to other cities and local species). What's next in Bettman's brave new NHL, driverless Zambonis?

BUDD LYNCH: The Windsor native, who lost his right arm in World War II and died in 2012, was the longtime PA man at The Joe, announcing line-ups, scoring plays, the last minute to play in periods and so on. Oh, to hear him say, "Viacheslav," one more time.

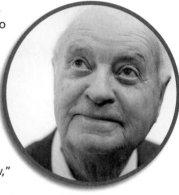

THE BROW: Before there was Mo Cheese, there was Joe Diroff in the '80s. He was a fan of all Detroit teams and known for his bushy eyebrows, white shirt and tie, bucket hat and props like mustard and ketchup bottles ("They can't cut the mustard!" and "They'll never catch up!").

MO CHEESE: That's the guy — just a fan in the stands — that cameras caught dancing in the stands when "The Curly Shuffle" was playing on the loudspeakers around the turn of the century. He became a mainstay, dancing during commercial breaks wearing a Wings jersey and Stanley Cup on his head.

MORE THAN JUST A HOME FOR THE RED WINGS, THE JOE PLAYED HOST TO CONCERTS, THE NBA AND WNBA, BOXING TITLE FIGHTS AND EVEN THE REPUBLICAN NATIONAL CONVENTION

STAR TURNS

FROM FREE PRESS STAFF OVER THE DECADES; EDITED BY GENE MYERS

NO. 1: JULY 16, 1980

THE GOP GATHERS IN THE MOTOR CITY

REAGAN PURSUES GERALD FORD AS RUNNING MATE, SETTLES FOR GEORGE H.W. BUSH, PROMISES 'TO MAKE AMERICA GREAT AGAIN'

The events that played out on the next-to-last day of the Republican National Convention changed the course of U.S. politics for at least three decades.

If a bold gambit by GOP nominee Ronald Reagan had succeeded, maybe he still would have defeated incumbent Jimmy Carter in November. But had Reagan's gambit succeeded, the odds of a Bush dynasty — George Herbert Walker Bush as the 41st president and his son George Walker Bush as the 43rd president — would have been miniscule.

In the spring of 1980, Reagan trailed Carter by roughly 20 points in the polls. Members of the Republican establishment feared Reagan was too old and too conservative; they believed Reagan was perfectly poised to lead the GOP to certain defeat. However, by the convention — ironically to be held in one of the country's most heavily Democratic cities — Reagan had made up ground in the polls. To strengthen the ticket, Reagan decided to pursue a former vice president (and president), Michigan's own Gerald Ford, to be his running mate. At least one poll had suggested that Ford would defeat Carter in a hypothetical showdown for the presidency.

A former president running to be vice president? It was the biggest story at a convention in eons. CBS led the charge throughout the day, and eventually said a Reagan-Ford ticket

was a done deal. ABC followed suit. During the evening, Ford fed the hype by visiting Walter Cronkite in the CBS anchor booth — while ABC's Barbara Walters waited outside — to tell America that if assured a "meaningful role" in a Reagan administration, he might consider the vice presidency. A "co-presidency," Cronkite termed the arrangement that Ford wanted.

However, negotiations between the former rivals for the 1976 GOP nomination collapsed late that night in Reagan's 69th-floor suite at the Detroit Plaza Hotel inside the Renaissance Center. Shortly before midnight, CBS and NBC reported that Ford was out and George H.W. Bush was in. The Free Press reported that Bush received his invitation at 11:37 p.m. By then, the Chicago Sun-Times had printed 120,000 copies with headlines about a Reagan-Ford ticket.

"When I left (Ford) after 5 p.m., it was still on," said Sen. Bob Dole, the Kansan who had been Ford's running mate in his failed 1976 campaign against Carter. "Maybe we left the wrong people in charge."

Bush, who during the primaries had called Reagan's supply-side policies "voodoo economics," downplayed being the second choice for the second spot. "What difference does it make?" he said. "I'm here because Gov.

CONTINUED ON PAGE 106

The Great Communicator

On the final night of the GOP convention, Ronald Reagan delivered a classic speech to fire up the faithful and throw down the gauntlet to President Jimmy Carter in the race ahead: "Let us dedicate ourselves to renewing the American compact. ... I ask you to trust that American spirit, which knows no ethnic, religious, social, political, regional or economic boundaries."

TONY SPINA/DETROIT FREE PRESS

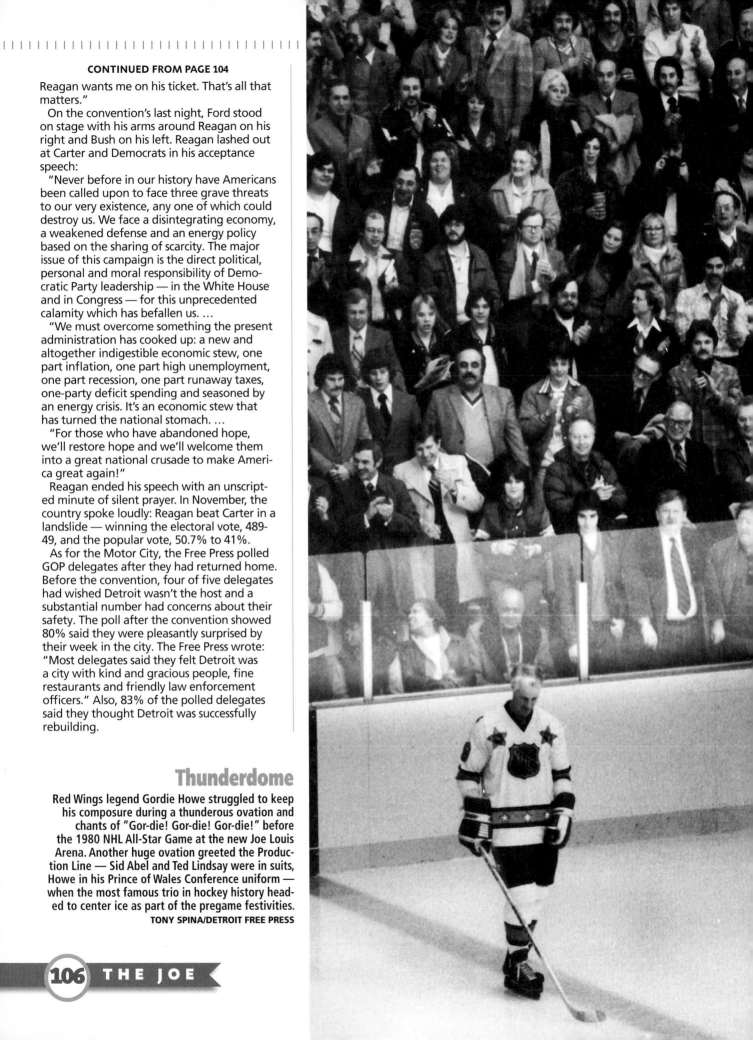

CONTINUED FROM PAGE 104

Reagan wants me on his ticket. That's all that matters."

On the convention's last night, Ford stood on stage with his arms around Reagan on his right and Bush on his left. Reagan lashed out at Carter and Democrats in his acceptance speech:

"Never before in our history have Americans been called upon to face three grave threats to our very existence, any one of which could destroy us. We face a disintegrating economy, a weakened defense and an energy policy based on the sharing of scarcity. The major issue of this campaign is the direct political, personal and moral responsibility of Democratic Party leadership — in the White House and in Congress — for this unprecedented calamity which has befallen us. …

"We must overcome something the present administration has cooked up: a new and altogether indigestible economic stew, one part inflation, one part high unemployment, one part recession, one part runaway taxes, one-party deficit spending and seasoned by an energy crisis. It's an economic stew that has turned the national stomach. …

"For those who have abandoned hope, we'll restore hope and we'll welcome them into a great national crusade to make America great again!"

Reagan ended his speech with an unscripted minute of silent prayer. In November, the country spoke loudly: Reagan beat Carter in a landslide — winning the electoral vote, 489-49, and the popular vote, 50.7% to 41%.

As for the Motor City, the Free Press polled GOP delegates after they had returned home. Before the convention, four of five delegates had wished Detroit wasn't the host and a substantial number had concerns about their safety. The poll after the convention showed 80% said they were pleasantly surprised by their week in the city. The Free Press wrote: "Most delegates said they felt Detroit was a city with kind and gracious people, fine restaurants and friendly law enforcement officers." Also, 83% of the polled delegates said they thought Detroit was successfully rebuilding.

Thunderdome

Red Wings legend Gordie Howe struggled to keep his composure during a thunderous ovation and chants of "Gor-die! Gor-die! Gor-die!" before the 1980 NHL All-Star Game at the new Joe Louis Arena. Another huge ovation greeted the Production Line — Sid Abel and Ted Lindsay were in suits, Howe in his Prince of Wales Conference uniform — when the most famous trio in hockey history headed to center ice as part of the pregame festivities.
TONY SPINA/DETROIT FREE PRESS

GORDIE HOWE COMES HOME

RECORD CROWD GOES WILD FOR MR. HOCKEY'S 23RD AND FINAL NHL ALL-STAR GAME

A few weeks shy of his 52nd birthday and now a right wing for the Hartford Whalers, Gordie Howe played in his 23rd and final NHL All-Star Game. The only midseason showcase played at The Joe would be a nod to the past — the legendary Howe was back in Detroit — and a glimpse to the future — a 19-year-old rookie sensation from a defunct league.

During his 26 NHL seasons, Howe missed an All-Star Game only once a decade (his 1947 rookie season, 1956 and 1966). His final one would include 14 future members of the Hockey Hall of Fame — and one already inducted member, Gordie. And it would include rookie Wayne Gretzky, who idolized Howe and would threaten in the decades to come to take his title as the greatest player ever.

Hockey's two greatest icons played against each other only because the World Hockey Association had folded the previous year. Howe retired from the Red Wings in 1971, had two frustrating years as a club executive, then Howe starred in the WHA for six years with Houston and New England, playing with sons Mark and Marty. Gretzky played for Indianapolis and Edmonton in the WHA in the 1978-79 season. After the league folded, Howe's Whalers and Gretzky's Oilers (along with Quebec and Winnipeg) were merged into the NHL.

A crowd of 21,002 jammed into The Joe to watch the Prince of Wales Conference beat the Campbell Conference, 6-3, setting an all-time attendance record — since broken — for a hockey game in North America.

The game always will be remembered for the thunderous standing ovation fans showered upon Howe. For the pregame introduction, announcer John Bell wisely introduced Howe last, but not by name. It was hardly necessary.

"And from the Hartford Whalers, representing all of hockey, the greatest statesman for five decades, No. 9!" Bell announced as the fans quickly rose to their feet.

Witnesses said it felt like a 20-minute ovation, but in reality, the crowd stood and cheered for 2½ minutes, chanting, "Gor-die! Gor-die! Gor-die!" until Bell interrupted the roar by introducing national anthem singers Roger Doucet and Roger Whittaker. Howe had skated in small circles on the blue line. "I felt like climbing into a hole," he said. "It was so embarrassing."

In an interview with Bill Dow for the Free Press 25 years later, Howe recalled: "I had the same feelings for the fans as they had towards me. I was very emotional, and the fans were getting to me, so I skated over to Lefty Wilson on the bench and asked for help so I would be normal again. Lefty was bilingual — he spoke English and profanity. He said something to me I can't repeat, and it worked."

Wilson was the Wings' trainer.

Every time Howe took a shift, the crowd cheered and chanted his name, hoping to see No. 9 turn the red light on again in Detroit.

Near the end of the first period, Howe received the puck at point-blank range in front of goalie Tony Esposito. Howe fired his famed snap shot at Esposito, who stopped the puck as the crowd groaned. The Blackhawks goalie promptly skated off the ice, having been injured by Howe's vicious shot.

"I wanted to shoot it low on his stick side, but I pulled it," Howe said. "I was unhappy with my performance because I missed that goal. I was nervous because I didn't want to make a fool of myself. Afterwards I wondered what the crowd would have done had I scored."

Later, a quick wrister from Howe was kicked away by rookie sensation Pete Peeters. Another wrister went wide.

But Howe's name would be announced again, prompting a final thunderous roar. Three minutes after Wings defenseman Reed Larson gave the Wales Conference a 5-3 lead, and with four minutes left in the game, Howe stole the puck twice before threading the needle on a perfect pass from behind the net. The puck went to Real Cloutier, who fired it past Peeters. Mr. Hockey was on the scoresheet with an assist — one more point than the Great One recorded.

NO. 3: APRIL 27, 1984

OH, ISIAH!

THOMAS' FINISH FOR THE AGES CAN'T SAVE THE PISTONS IN A PLAYOFF THRILLER

"It was a night when the Pistons came back to Detroit, a night when urban ball replaced suburban ball, a night when a bunch of guys shooting baskets turned 21,208 men, women and children into basket cases."

Free Press columnist Mike Downey wrote those words after the Pistons lost the decisive game of a first-round series with the New York Knicks in overtime. In many ways, the final score was the least interesting of the story lines that played out on a Friday night at The Joe. And we're not just talking about Isiah Thomas' legendary 16 points in 93 seconds down the stretch.

For starters, why were the Pistons even playing at The Joe? It wasn't because a snowstorm caved in the Silverdome's inflatable roof, although that's what happened the following winter. The Pistons were displaced because the Silverdome had been filled with dirt for a motocross. "Didn't they think we were going to be in the playoffs?" coach Chuck Daly complained. Well, yes, that was it exactly.

In their previous six seasons, the Pistons had missed the playoffs each year. In their previous 21 seasons, the Pistons had won only one playoff series. The joke was that the Pistons were a team without a history. That wouldn't change until the late 1980s when Thomas and the Bad Boys would write one.

Games 1 and 2 of the Pistons-Knick series drew a little more than 14,000 fans to the Silverdome. After the Pistons won Game 4, 119-112, in Madison Square Garden, tickets to the decisive Game 5 sold like hoop-shaped hotcakes. George Blaha, the voice of the Pistons, dubbed it the "Showdown in Motown." George Puscas, longtime Free Press columnist, called it "the most important game of the franchise's life."

The Joe was ungodly hot the night of Game 5. Daly wondered: "Is it always so hot in here?" Downey wrote: "No. If it was, several Red Wings would have drowned."

CONTINUED ON PAGE 108

CONTINUED FROM PAGE 107

Downey also wrote: "Maybe three times as many black basketball fans came around than had come to a typical game at the Silverdome."

On the court, the Pistons and Knicks engaged in a bitter, physical, back-and-forth battle. "It was like a 15-round championship fight," Daly said, "and the guy on his feet at the end wins."

When Thomas sat the final 6:52 of the third quarter, the Pistons managed only two baskets until his return. So the Knicks carried an 85-79 lead into the final quarter. When Bernard King scored his 34th point with about two minutes to play, the Knicks' lead stood at eight points, 106-98.

Then Thomas went crazy. He pushed the ball up the court, took one dribble behind his back and hit a jumper in the lane — 106-100 with 1:56 to play. He hit another jumper from the line, drew a foul from Rory Sparrow and made the free throw — 108-103. He stole the ball from Sparrow and drew a loose ball foul on him. He traded points with the Knicks again — 110-105.

Thomas was fouled by Sparrow yet again attempting a jumper just outside the lane. He made one free throw — 110-106 with 58 seconds left. He drove almost the entire length of the court, weaved through all five Knicks in the lane, drew a foul and hit a lay-up. He made the free throw — 112-109 with 45 seconds left.

Pressured by Kelly Tripucka deep in the backcourt, New York's Louis Orr stepped on the sideline. Thomas then hit a jumper in the lane — 112-111 with 35 seconds left. After King hit a jumper for the Knicks, Thomas had the crowd dancing and clapping in the aisles when his picture-perfect three-pointer cut cleanly through the nets to tie it at 114 with 23 seconds left.

"Sometimes Zeke is magical," Daly would say. "Only he can play like that."

When John Long harassed Darrell Walker into botching an inbounds pass, the Pistons got the ball back, still with 23 seconds left. Thomas had a chance for the best two minutes since Secretariat.

He stood at the top of the key; his teammates fanned out to the sides. Walker, a terrific defender, watched and waited for the move he knew was sure to come: Thomas driving for the hoop. When he did, Walker slapped the ball away in the lane with four seconds left.

In overtime, Bill Laimbeer's fallaway jumper gave the Pistons a 116-114 lead. But they missed their next 11 shots. Laimbeer fouled out. The Knicks went up by seven, 123-116.

Then Thomas struck again, with a long bomb and a lay-up. Earl Cureton's lay-up made it a 125-123 deficit with a minute to go.

The magic ended with 37 seconds left: Thomas fouled Bill Cartwright under the basket. It was his sixth foul. Cartwright made two free throws. The final score was 127-123.

Thomas finished with 35 points on 13-for-25 shooting. Tripucka added 23 points and Laimbeer 17 rebounds. King scored 44 points — his fourth straight 40-plus playoff game. He did it despite sitting eight minutes in the third quarter with his fourth foul, suffering from the flu and battling two dislocated fingers. He went 17-for-26 from the field and 10-for-13 from the line and grabbed 12 rebounds.

"I'll never forget this game," Tripucka said. And he knew what to do with his sudden time off: "I guess I'll drink beer, eat Wendy's and get fat again."

Grace on ice

On the practice rink at Cobo Arena, shortly before being attacked, Nancy Kerrigan worked on her routine for the following night's short program. Her coach, Evy Scotvold, said: "I feel very sad for the skating community in Detroit. I've worked with them for years and years and they are one of the best skating towns in America. This is probably going to bother them so much, but it wasn't their fault."
WILLIAM ARCHIE/DETROIT FREE PRESS

FIGURE SKATING BECOMES A CONTACT SPORT
AN UNKNOWN ASSAILANT WHACKS KERRIGAN'S KNEE AND THE SKATING WORLD GOES NUTS

"The Whack Heard 'Round The World" didn't happen at The Joe. It actually occurred in a corridor at Cobo Arena, which connects to The Joe, right after women competing for figure skating berths in the Lillehammer Olympics had a practice session.

But for the initial days of insanity that followed The Whack, The Joe was the epicenter for what at first appeared to be an attack by a skating fanatic but what really turned out to be a surreal, almost comic, story of jealousy, vengeance and deceit.

The saga of Tonya Harding — the bad girl who smokes and likes to roughhouse with boys — and Nancy Kerrigan — the good girl who's dainty and elegant and now America's Victim — captivated the nation's attention for seven weeks. During the Olympics, nearly half the U.S. households watched the prime-time broadcast of the women's short program, even though it had ended hours earlier. Only the last episode of "M*A*S*H," the "Who Shot J.R.?" episode of "Dallas," an episode of "Roots" and two Super Bowls scored higher ratings.

Ten days before Kerrigan was clubbed on the knee at Cobo, four men with connections to Harding met 1,300 miles away in Portland, Ore. Among them was her on-again, off-again husband, Jeff Gillooly, and her sometime bodyguard, Shawn Eckhardt. One man said: "Why don't we just kill her, or set up a car wreck?" Another said: "We don't need to kill her. Let's just hit her in the knee." And that's how a $6,500 plot was hatched to keep Kerrigan, the 1992 Olympic bronze medalist, from winning the U.S. championships in Detroit and a gold medal in Lillehammer.

"The amateur hit men would leave behind a paper and electronic trail so obvious that Mr. Magoo could have solved this mystery," the Free Press later wrote in a three-page tick-tock article about the scheme. "They made calls through hotel switchboards, checked in under their own names and wired money through Western Union. They invented alibis that wouldn't fool anyone."

A day before the short program — it was a Thursday afternoon — Kerrigan was the last skater to leave the Cobo rink. As she walked in her skate guards through a blue curtain into a hallway leading to the locker room, a large man named Shane Stant in a black leather coat and a black hat ran toward her from behind. In one motion, without saying a word, he swung a metal baton that whacked her right knee. She collapsed and let out three ear-piercing shrieks. Stant bolted out of the hall and used his forehead to break through a Plexiglass door and escape into a snowstorm. "It hurts. It hurts so bad. I'm scared," Kerrigan cried to her father, Dan, who rushed to her side. "Why me? Why now? Help me! Help me! Please get my skate off."

A trip to Hutzel Hospital revealed a severely bruised and swollen knee, but nothing that probably wouldn't heal in a reasonable time frame. From the Westin Hotel, Kerringan told ABC during that night's events at The Joe: "I don't lose faith in all people. That's just one bad guy. … This has happened in other sports." More than 40 flower bouquets and scores of faxes and letters were delivered to the Westin for Kerrigan.

The following morning, blood was drained from Kerrigan's knee and she withdrew from the competition. Technically, that made her ineligible for the Olympic team, but a little rule-bending was in the works. Harding led after Friday's short program and the next night celebrated her second ladies national championship. Kerrigan, who watched from a skybox, was awarded the second and final Olympic spot.

"I'm not going away with anything less than gold," Harding vowed. "I'm going to whip her butt!"

Within days, a new scenario emerged: Forget about Kerrigan's injury; would Harding be allowed on the U.S. team?

Before Harding's and Gillooly's return to Portland, their complicity in the attack started to become apparent to Detroit police and then the FBI.

An unknown older woman, sounding scared, called Detroit police long distance Sunday morning and wanted to pass a tip only to deputy chief Benny Napoleon, who had appeared regularly on national television to answer questions about the investigation. Napoleon was at home sleeping when his beeper went off. Within minutes, the woman told him that she had heard a tape recording of Eckhardt and another man plotting an attack. Napoleon and chief Ike McKinnon immediately called the FBI.

In Portland the same day, a minister told the FBI about a tape Eckart, now guilt stricken, played for him of the attack-planning meeting.

Three days later, Eckhardt and Derrick Smith, the fourth man at the meeting and Stant's uncle, gave the FBI signed confessions for their roles in the scheme. Two days after that, Stant also confessed.

On Jan. 19, 13 days after that fateful day at Cobo, Gillooly was charged with planning and bankrolling the attack. Police reports linked Harding to the plot for the first time. Eckhardt had told authorities that Harding skated up to him at a practice and declared: "You know, you need to stop screwing around with this and get it done." Harding, in turn, announced that she and Gillooly were separating again, despite continuing to wear his ring.

But a grand jury did not indict Harding then. She battled and threatened and managed to keep her place on the Olympic team. She finished eighth in Norway but won an unofficial gold medal for drama. In the long program, she said she cut a lace during warm-ups, didn't have time to replace it and tried to skate her routine anyway. When she couldn't complete a jump, she broke down in tears, showed her skate to the judges and begged for a do-over. They agreed. She delivered a decent program, smiled at the end and blew a kiss to the crowd. "I left my problems behind," she said.

Temporarily. She pleaded guilty to a felony charge of hindering the prosecution. She avoided jail but was banished from skating. Gillooly, Eckhardt, Stant and Smith all went to prison.

As for Kerrigan, she lost the gold to Ukraine's Oksana Baiul by the narrowest of margins. "I thought I had won," Kerrigan said. "I thought I skated great."

On the 20th anniversary of "The Whack Heard 'Round The World," USA TODAY's Christine Brennan interviewed the bitter rivals.

Kerrigan: "I really don't look back unless someone asks me to look back, and then I have to. Otherwise, why would I? I was attacked."

Harding: "I know it was a horrible time for everyone involved. It was a bad streak, going through all the crud, and I was able to rise above it. I think Nancy and I have good lives."

Kerrigan said she had not seen or spoken with Harding. "Never. No. For what?"

THE HITMAN COMETH

LANKY HEARNS CAPTURES HIS FIRST BELT

Detroit's young (all of 21) and unbeaten (28-0 with 26 KOs) Hitman, Thomas Hearns, unleashed a stunning barrage on defenseless Pipino Cuevas, then knocked out the Mexican with an awesome right to the head in the second round to capture the World Boxing Association's welterweight championship.

The end came with Cuevas struggling to his knees, looking blankly out at an electrified crowd at The Joe as referee Stanley Christodoulou began to count him out. He never completed the formality. Cuevas' manager, Lupe Sanchez, recognizing instantly that his fighter was finished, climbed through the ring ropes, signaled an end to the fight and reached out to help Cuevas, the champion since 1976.

Pandemonium seized the crowd. Dozens stormed into the ring. Hearns had completed an odyssey that in just 2½ years took him from the city's east-side ghetto to the top of his game.

"That's exactly the way we planned it," said Kronk's Emanuel Steward, manager of Hearns and lightweight champion Hilmer Kenty, who successfully defended his title with a ninth-round TKO over South Korea's Yung Ho Oh. "It was about as perfect as you can plot anything and have it turn out."

The hype for Hearns-Cuevas was off the charts. That's why the Free Press offered two $500 ringside tickets in a poetry contest. CKLW-AM (800) disc jockey Dick Purtan, Kenty and Hearns were the judges. Out of more than 10,000 entries, Jerry Czarnecki of Livonia won for this:

The showdown in Motown
Will go down in history
As the night Pipino
Got a lesson in fistory.

And that's why, after the fact, Free Press columnist Jim Hawkins called the bout "the most marvelous night of boxing in modern Motor City history."

"Hearns is a very good fighter," Cuevas said, "and I hope he will be as good a champion as I was."

He was. Hearns would become the first fighter to win world titles in four weight divisions and then added a fifth, and he twice was Ring magazine's fighter of the year. Steward would become known as a master trainer, first for his work with his stable of Detroit talent at Kronk Gym and then as a hired gun for boxing's best around the globe.

The legend, the artist, his tub ...

Yes, that's a clawfoot bathtub. The music video for "When Doves Cry" opened with Prince reclining in the tub. According to BuzzFeed: "The tub was also part of the set for his Purple Rain Tour, in which it would emerge ... using a hydraulic lift. But during a final dress rehearsal, the tub carrying Prince wasn't secured tightly on the lift and both fell to the ground. 'Everybody rushed over and checked him out,' keyboardist Matt Fink said in (the book) 'Let's Go Crazy,' 'and fortunately, nothing had broken, but he was bruised pretty badly.'"

WILLIAM ARCHIE/DETROIT FREE PRESS

The power of purple

For seven concerts, Prince fans packed The Joe for the start of the Purple Rain Tour. "There was something about Prince's music that just resonated with Detroit," Ted Joseph, the Detroit promotion manager for Warner Bros. Records during the singer's early days, told the Free Press after Prince's death in 2016. "The people of Detroit gravitated to his music like nobody else did, before other cities jumped on the bandwagon."
WILLIAM ARCHIE/DETROIT FREE PRESS

NO. 6: NOV. 4, 1984
REIGN OF 'RAIN'
PRINCE AND HIS NEW BAND OPEN LEGENDARY TOUR

Prince Rogers Nelson, the latest heir to the American rock 'n' roll hysteria that started with Elvis Presley, arrived at The Joe on the heels of the No. 1 movie in the country ("Purple Rain"), the No. 1 album in the country ("Purple Rain") and the No. 1 single in the country ("Purple Rain"). The mania for Prince's aptly named Purple Rain Tour was so great that nearly 300 reporters, including delegations from Europe, Japan and Australia, and enough photographers to fill the two penalty boxes covered the tour's start at The Joe, the first of seven sold-out shows in nine nights.

Why the Motor City? Although born in Minneapolis, Minn., Prince came to regard Detroit as a second hometown. It embraced his music long before white audiences noticed him and long before he became a global superstar. He was a frequent visitor by the early '80s, including a six-show stand at the Masonic Temple in 1982.

"Starting the tour here is a statement of the appreciation to the people of Detroit for the undying support given to all Prince-related projects from the beginning to today," said Chuck DeBow, marketing director for Prince's managers.

After Sheila E. opened at The Joe, Prince and The Revolution — his backing band finally had an official name, plus new guitarist Wendy Melvoin — rewarded the faithful with a flashy light show, costume changes, an elevated purple bathtub and a repertoire heavy on songs from the chart-topping "Purple Rain." Critics considered this album among the greatest of all time.

The Free Press' Gary Graff wrote: "They stood from the second the arena went dark, and they screamed at the first chair-shaking synthesizer chord. By the time Prince, standing atop a bank of speakers, intoned, 'Detroit — my name is Prince, and I've come to play with you,' they were ready to accept anything."

The show started with "Let's Go Crazy," included "When Doves Cry" and ended with — what else? — "Purple Rain."

WANDERING WINNERS

BOOTED FROM THE PALACE, SHOCK CAPTURES ANOTHER WNBA CROWN

At tip-off, roughly 8,000 Detroit Shock fans were seated for the decisive game of the WNBA Finals against the defending champion Sacramento Monarchs. But the box office line stretched to the parking lot. By halftime, The Joe was sold out and rocking with 19,671 fans.

"These fans came out," guard Katie Smith said, "and really got us going."

Well, at least in the second half. The Shock was down eight points at intermission and playing poorly, but with the stands now packed, Detroit erased the halftime deficit in 2½ minutes. Deanna Nolan, after a 4-for-13 half, hit her first five shots in the third quarter. Next thing you knew, the Shock had gone on a 22-9 run, and the building borrowed from the Red Wings for a day, because the Palace was booked for a Mariah Carey concert, was shaking from the noise. Forward Cheryl Ford, who had 10 points and 10 rebounds, said it made her "claustrophobic." The lead grew to 13 points in the fourth quarter.

A hush fell over the crowd with 33.2 seconds left, though, after a late Sacramento charge cut the lead to 78-75. Then Smith dribbled to her left, trying to kill some clock, before she drained a 17-foot jumper — the title clincher — with 14.8 seconds left. "That's what I do," said Smith, borrowing a line from the Pistons' Rip Hamilton. "I score buckets." Final score: Shock 80, Monarchs 75.

Smith scored 13 of her 17 points in the second half. Nolan, who won the Miss Basketball Award at Flint Northern, received the Finals MVP award after scoring 24 points in Game 5.

The players mobbed each other at midcourt. Kara Braxton cradled her 1½-year-old son, Jalani, in her arms. Swin Cash and Ford, who both played on the Shock's 2003 championship team, stood forehead-against-forehead with Cash yelling, "Two! Two! Two!"

The locker room smelled of champagne, sweat and Colt 45. Players took turns abusing Cash's teddy bear, Shocka, whom she took almost everywhere. Assistant coach Rick Mahorn poured his malt liquor on Shocka's head. "Shocka's 30," he explained to Cash. "Shocka needs some 45." Cash couldn't protect her bear because she was trying to protect her hair from the spray of Silver Cap champagne. "Y'all don't know how much this weave costs!" she yelled. Braxton, sipping a 40-ouncer of Colt 45, dumped it on Cash's head.

Owner Bill Davidson, who received the championship trophy during the ESPN2 broadcast, said he reminded coach Bill Laimbeer that "part of my job description is accepting trophies." Mr. D's trophy tally: three NBA, two WNBA and one Stanley Cup (with Tampa Bay).

Davidson's Shock would win his final trophy in 2008. He died the following spring, and by the fall his widow, Karen Davidson, had sold the Shock to an interest in Tulsa, Okla.

Another win for Swin

The Shock drafted forward Swin Cash with the second selection in 2002, after her undefeated season at Connecticut, and she became the face of the franchise off the court and turned around its woebegone fortunes on the court. She won WNBA titles in 2003 and, despite an ailing back, in 2006. But Cash was traded before the 2008 title season because of a rocky relationship with coach Bill Laimbeer.

AMY LEANG/DETROIT FREE PRESS

NO. 8: AUG. 11, 1990
KINGS OF THE ARENA
WITH A BUSTED BUCKEYE AT THE HELM, THE DRIVE MOTORS TO A THREE-PEAT IN THE AFL

In the 1950s, the Lions were an NFL dynasty, winning three championships and losing in the title game once. In 1983, the Michigan Panthers won the first USFL championship. But no Detroit pro football team ever dominated like the Drive of the Arena Football League. In its six seasons — 1988-93 — the Mike Ilitch-owned Drive played in the ArenaBowl each time and won four times.

The zenith for the Drive came in 1990, when a banished Buckeye played the game of his life and 19,875 fans howled with joy as the team completed a three-peat. Art Schlichter, the 30-year-old former All-America quarterback from Ohio State, ran for four touchdowns and passed for two more in a 51-27 victory over the Dallas Texans. In the Drive's third season, it had won its third championship.

Schlichter famously battled a gambling addiction as a pro. The fourth pick in the 1982 draft, by the Colts, he had been suspended, reinstated and waived for good in 1985 when he resumed gambling. His résumé after that included part of a season in the Canadian Football League, a conviction for involvement in a sports betting operation, filing for bankruptcy and commissioner Pete Rozelle saying he couldn't return to the NFL. Schlichter returned to pro football — the 50-yard version, at least — with the Drive in 1990 and won the league's MVP award.

"Playing here really taught me a lot about football," he said, "and Mike Ilitch has offered me a fine opportunity."

Against the Texans, Schlichter scored on two short runs in the game's first seven minutes. His 11-yard touch-

Ilitch's other dynasty

Long gone from Detroit, the Drive's short-but-sweet history was summed up in one banner that hung at The Joe. After the Drive won its fourth title, a 56-38 victory at Orlando in 1992, coach Tim Marcum said: "I love the fans of Detroit. … We know we're not a big sport around here, but people treat us like we are."
DETROIT FREE PRESS

down pass to Alvin Rettig made it 28-0 with 9:36 left in the half. Dallas made it a game at 28-14, until Novo Bojovic kicked a 42-yard field goal to end the half and Schlichter scored on a one-yard run to start the second.

"We've got the best players in our league — ain't that obvious?" defensive end John Corker laughed as he sprayed his teammates with champagne. "Tell the Pistons that we're pulling for them to be the second Detroit team to three-peat! … But they're after us."

Corker, who like Bojovic had played on the Panthers' championship team, later was inducted into the AFL Hall of Fame. Like his teammates, he received a $500 bonus as a league champion, plus another $500 Ilitch threw in.

Schlichter returned for the 1991 season, but the Drive lost, 48-42, to Tampa Bay in ArenaBowl V. Soon after, his life spiraled out of control again, as he gambled away his earnings, stole or conned his way to get more money, passed bad checks and bounced in and out of jail. In 2007, he told ESPN he estimated he had stolen at least $1.5 million. In 2011, he was sentenced to 10 years for a ticket scam plus additional time for testing positive for cocaine while under house arrest.

The Drive won its final title in 1992, shortly after Ilitch acquired the Detroit Tigers. He sold the Drive the next year, the franchise moved to Worcester as the Massachusetts Marauders and folded after one season.

The final line: The Drive went 46-10 (.821) in the regular season and 12-2 (.857) in the playoffs. Joining Corker in the Hall of Fame are Ilitch, general manager Gary Vitto, coaches Tim Marcum and Perry Moss, and a host of players, including wide receiver/defensive back George LaFrance (MVP in 1989 and '90), wide receiver/linebacker Dwayne Dixon and two-way lineman Jon Roehlk.

NO. 9: DEC. 29, 1982
THAT OLD COLLEGE TRY
VICTORY FOR MSU! ATTENDANCE RECORD FOR THE JOE! LOUDEST FANS SINCE 1968!

The box office shut down at 6:30 p.m., 90 minutes before the championship game of the 18th Great Lakes Invitational college hockey tournament. Then Michigan State, ranked fourth in the nation, beat Michigan Tech, 5-3, before 21,347 raucous, screaming fans, a record for a hockey game in North America.

Tom Henderson wrote for Free Press:

"The news of this night was the crowd — the largest ever to see a hockey game, barring something bigger behind the Iron Curtain; the largest crowd in the young history of Joe Louis; probably the loudest crowd around here since most of Michigan poured downtown to celebrate the Tigers' World Series win in 1968."

The following December, fourth-ranked MSU beat Tech again for the title, 6-2, before 21,402 fans, upping the record by 55. And December 1984, when top-ranked MSU beat Tech yet again for the title, 7-0, the promoters announced a crowd of 21,576. Through the end of 2016, no crowd at The Joe ever would be bigger.

OPENING ACTS

Rush performed the first concert at Joe Louis Arena in February 1980. Kid Rock, born in Romeo, Mich., signed to play the first concert at the new Little Caesars Arena in September 2017. Other first musical acts in Detroit venues:

OLYMPIA STADIUM: Ted Lewis Orchestra, Jan. 23, 1942.

BRIGGS STADIUM: "Star Night," July 23, 1954. Featuring Ray Anthony, Mitchell Ayres, Archie Bleyer, Nat King Cole, Perry Como, Jill Corey, Roy Hamilton, Julius La Rose, Ralph Marterie, Patti Page and Sarah Vaughan.

COBO ARENA: Jerry Lee Lewis, May 17, 1961.

TIGER STADIUM: Rod Stewart, Sept. 25, 1993.

PONTIAC SILVERDOME: The Who, Dec. 6, 1975.

PALACE OF AUBURN HILLS: Sting, Aug. 13, 1988.

COMERICA PARK: Dave Matthews Band, July 5, 2000.

FORD FIELD: The Rolling Stones and No Doubt, Oct. 12, 2002.

We fought the law ... and the law won

Detroit police brandishing nightsticks finally tamed an unruly early-morning crowd that had stormed Cobo Arena in an attempt to purchase Rush tickets. "They were all trying to get in first," Sgt. Stacy Brackens said. The Free Press pointed out in its photo caption that this "rock fan ... was not arrested."
WILLIAM ARCHIE/DETROIT FREE PRESS

NO. 10: FEB. 17, 1980

IN A RUSH

RUSH STAGES THE FIRST CONCERT IN DETROIT'S NEW RIVERFRONT ARENA, BUT NOT WITHOUT A FEW HARROWING MOMENTS IN TICKET SALES

A modern-day warrior.
Mean, mean stride.
Today's Tom Sawyer.
Mean, mean pride.

The first concerts at The Joe featured Rush, the Canadian progressive rock trio that packed venues throughout the Detroit area for decades. In fact, its Permanent Waves tour, from Aug. 17, 1979, through June 22, 1980, included five concerts in the metro area, Aug. 27 at Cobo Arena in Detroit, Aug. 28 at Pine Knob Music Theatre in Clarkston, Sept. 10 at Pine Knob and Feb. 17 and 19 at Joe Louis Arena. (On Feb. 18, the Wings hosted the Kings — a 4-2 loss that extended a winless streak to seven games — so Rush played outside Cleveland in the Richfield Coliseum.)

The concerts at The Joe were a big hit with fans. One review declared that the new arena "does the job for concerts" and "the sound reproduction is almost identical to that of Cobo."

However, ticket sales were a near disaster for the opener. On Jan. 12, 1980, the Free Press wrote that "an unruly crowd of young rock music fans" rushed the ticket office at Cobo, broke the glass in six doors and tore two doors off their hinges. Numerous fans were knocked to the ground or pinned against walls, fearful they would be stomped or crushed to death. (A month earlier, 11 people had been

killed in Cincinnati before a Who concert when fans rushed into the arena for general-admission seating.)

Around 8:30 a.m., a rumor had spread at Cobo that there were not enough tickets — at 10 a.m. 20,029 tickets were to go on sale for $9, $10 and $11 — for the 1,500 or so people in the line, many who had waited all night in temperatures in the low teens and gusty winds and steeled themselves with marijuana, beer and other alcoholic beverages. Eight police officers were on duty at Cobo and more than dozen were called to the scene within minutes, according to the Free Press. United Press International placed the total number of officers at 50. They brandished nightsticks — witnesses said they hit fans in the legs to move them back — and maintained strict order the rest of the morning. No injuries were reported, although one arrest for disorderly conduct was made.

First on The Joe's stage in February was Max Webster, a band that hailed from Toronto like Rush. The headliners — vocalist and keyboardist Geddy Lee, guitarist Alex Lifeson and drummer Neil Peart — played a 20-song concert, starting with "2112," including "Xanadu" and "Cygnus X-1: Book II: Hemispheres" and ending with "La Villa Strangiato." For the record, the trio did not record "Tom Sawyer," its staple of classic rock radio, until later in 1980.

Super rock friends

In 2006, Detroit music icons Kid Rock and Bob Seger wowed The Joe with "Rock & Roll Never Forgets." Rock said he had planned this show way back in 2000, as soon as the city got word it would be hosting Super Bowl XL. In his review of Rock's concert, Brian McCollum wrote for the Free Press: "In a week stuffed with splashy parties and all manner of hyperbole, Friday night at The Joe stood out. With velvet ropes and snarling bouncers taking over the rest of the city, this was a party Detroit threw for itself."
ROMAIN BLANQUART/DETROIT FREE PRESS

NO. 11: FEB. 3, 2006

THE DEVIL WITHOUT A CAUSE

SEGER, KID ROCK TEAM UP FOR A DETROIT ROCK CITY PARTY AHEAD OF SUPER BOWL XL

Although the Pittsburgh Steelers beat the Seattle Seahawks in the big game at Ford Field, 21-10, the defining moment of Super Bowl week for thousands of Michiganders happened at The Joe. On Friday and Saturday nights, Kid Rock, who took the stage in typical over-the-top style with a black fedora and a full-length fur coat, performed sold-out shows that featured Bob Seger as his surprise guest.

The Free Press' Brian McCollum wrote: "OK, see, this is how Detroit throws a party. Detroit takes a Friday night, puts a bunch of loud people in a place called Joe Louis Arena, and sticks Bob Seger on-stage with Kid Rock for an electric rock 'n' roll moment that those 17,000 people aren't going to forget.

"With the sort of fanfare appropriate for a fanfare-heavy week in Detroit, the rarely seen Seger — 60 years old and introduced by Rock as 'the king of Detroit rock city' — joined the 35-year-old Rock for a duet on Seger's high-energy '70s chestnut, 'Rock & Roll Never Forgets.' …

"The pairing was brief but notable: Rock and Seger have become close friends — a tight relationship that bridges two generations of Detroit music."

ALPHABET CITY

RKO, HHH AND A ROYAL RUMBLE PLAY TO WRESTLING'S ENDURING APPEAL AT THE JOE

Over the decades, whether for routine or big-time events, pro wrestling played to packed houses at The Joe.

In 1987, Ric (Nature Boy) Flair lost his NWA championship belt to Ron Garvin in a cage match. They had been feuding over Flair's lust for Precious, the valet for Jimmy Garvin, Ron's brother. With a victory over Jimmy, Flair won a date with Precious, but his date turned out to be Miss Atlanta Lively, really Ron Garvin in drag.

You can't make this stuff up!

In 2016, Michigan football coach Jim Harbaugh, a huge wrestling fan who considered Flair his all-time favorite, sat ringside for WWE Raw and, when introduced, he jumped up and started waving his arms to fire up the crowd. Of course the clip went viral on the Internet.

Fans will never forget WWE's 22nd Royal Rumble in 2009, a pay-per-view extravaganza shown around the world. In the 30-man rumble match, wrestlers are eliminated by being thrown from the ring. Randy Orton, the eighth wrestler to enter the ring, won by last eliminating Triple H, the seventh entrant, after 58 minutes and 37 seconds of

mayhem and chaos. The last six wrestlers in the ring were The Big Show, The Undertaker, Triple H (pictured to the left) and The Legacy (Cody Rhodes, Ted DiBiase and Orton). While The Big Show and The Undertaker fought outside the ropes on the apron, Orton eliminated Big Show with an RKO (that slang for Randy Keith Orton's finishing move that starts with a two-handed grab of an opponent's neck and ends with a head slam to the ground). Big Show, although eliminated, pulled down Undertaker — and they continued fighting outside the ring. The Legacy ganged up to attack Triple H, who miraculously rallied to eliminate DiBiase and then Rhodes. With Triple H's back to Orton, Orton rushed him and threw him over the ropes by his head and shoulders.

Also in the match were Shelton Benjamin, Carlito, Jim Duggan, Fit Finlay, Goldust, Great Khali, Mark Henry, Chris Jericho, JTG, Kane, Brian Kendrick, Kofi Kingston, Mike Knox, Vladimir Kozlov, Santino Marella, The Miz, John Morrison, MVP, Rey Mysterio, CM Punk, William Regal, R-Truth, Rob Van Dam and Dolph Ziggler.

Big Sean, big spectacle

In November 2015, besides pulling together all the artists from "Detroit vs. Everybody," Big Sean delivered "his most cohesive, taut Detroit performance yet," Brian McCollum wrote in his Free Press review. "In front of a diverse crowd that came with energy on full tilt, he took the stage atop a set fashioned like an inner-city street block, flanked by a live band and DJ Mo Beatz. ... It was a two-hour display of mutual affection between Big Sean and his Detroit audience, replete with 'family' references and hometown pride."

TIM GALLOWAY/DETROIT FREE PRESS

DETROIT VS. EVERYBODY

THE NIGHT MOTOWN'S RAP ROYALTY JOINED FORCES FOR BIG SEAN

Tell 'em if they want it, they can come get that
I swear I love my city, I just want a little
See me, they salute me, they ain't ready for that
Detroit vs. Everybody

Detroit rapper Big Sean, the Cass Tech graduate coming off his first No. 1 album, "Dark Sky Paradise," called it "the best day of my life." Not only did he deliver a knockout concert at The Joe, but also he pulled together the hometown heavyweights of hip hop to perform "Detroit vs. Everybody." The joint effort with Eminem, Royce da 5'9", Danny Brown, Dej Loaf and Trick Trick — one year to the week after the Motor City anthem's release — was instant viral material around the globe, grabbing headlines and lighting up social media. In The Joe, the surprise gathering of rap royalty spurred crowd roars that often drowned out the music.

"Fifty years from now," Big Sean said, "I'll still remember that night."

Before the concert's capstone, Dej Loaf, Mike Posner, Jhene Aiko and Lil Wayne performed with Big Sean on stage.

Arranging the six-artist "Detroit vs. Everybody" was a months-long dance. "Eminem hasn't performed in 2015 at all," Big Sean said of the rapper long known for being reclusive and selective, not the sort of star given to guest cameos. "He's a legend — honestly, sometimes I feel like I'm talking to a ghost, how legendary he is. He's here, and then he just disappears."

Big Sean said he was nervous before the concert, a rarity for him. An afternoon rehearsal didn't help ease the jitters. "I kept fumbling because it was such a moment for me," he said. "I had so many things in my head, I couldn't remember my verse. I couldn't think of the words. Eminem was there, under the stage, waiting to pop out from underground. I'm just sitting there thinking, 'Wow, I'm onstage with Royce da 5'9", and Eminem is about to pop up.' It was a major moment for me. But I executed it in the show perfectly, and that's what counts."

NO. 14: JUNE 19, 1989

STRAIGHT OUTTA THE JOE

LEGENDARY RAPPERS N.W.A. MAKE A STAND FOR FREE SPEECH AT THE JOE, BUT THE CONTROVERSY ENSUES ALL THE WAY TO THE SILVER SCREEN

For several weeks in the summer of 2015, "Straight Outta Compton" was the No. 1 movie at the box office. Straight Outta The Joe played a supporting role because of a famous N.W.A. concert in 1989.

In the movie, the rappers are warned not to perform "F--- tha Police." One very stern officer says, "Just watch yourself." But the rappers start the song anyway, because even though N.W.A. billed itself as "The World's Most Dangerous Group," it never compromised on the Bill of Rights. Before long, the cops chased Ice Cube, Dr. Dre, Eazy-E, DJ Yella and MC Ren out of the arena and threw them into a police van.

Movie biopics tend to condense and reshape historical events and may even present alternative facts. So, what exactly went down in Motown remains open to dispute.

At the time, the Free Press described a heavy police presence around The Joe, reported that nine adults and nine juveniles were arrested on misdemeanor charges and quoted James Bannon, executive deputy police chief, as saying N.W.A. began its profanely titled song even though the promoters agreed it would not be included. "The song was not finished and band representatives couldn't be reached to explain why," the story said.

A few months later, London's Guardian wrote that police stormed the stage and "the band was escorted to their hotel by more officers, one of whom reportedly said, 'We just wanted to show the kids that you can't say, "F--- the police" in Detroit.'"

Former band manager Jerry Heller's memoir included yet another version: "The members of N.W.A. were hustled away from the arena by their security and whisked off to the safety of their hotel rooms — only to be arrested later when they sneaked down to the lobby to meet girls."

After the movie's release, a retired Detroit sergeant, Larry Courts, gave his version of events at a Black Lives Do Matter community forum in Ypsilanti. According to mlive.com, Courts said: "I was working the gang squad at the time. Those types of venues, we were always there. … There were close to 200 of us." Courts said he disagreed with the decision to prevent N.W.A. from performing "F--- tha Police" because "this is America," but "we had our marching orders."

Courts said he personally told the rappers they couldn't play the song. "At the end of their performance," he recalled, "they started their song. We immediately jumped on stage and started taking out amplifiers. … That's when the problem started."

Concert scenes for "Straight Outta Compton" were shot in Los Angeles and Santa Monica, Calif., but some filming took place in Detroit for The Joe scene, according to Universal.

"I WOULDN'T HAVE COME OUT TO SEE ANYONE TONIGHT — EVEN ME!"

FRANK SINATRA, who toasted the 12,000-14,000 fans who braved the snow to watch him at The Joe on Feb. 3, 1982

Making cars, making memories

Bob Seger brought the crowd to its feet with his third number, "Making Thunderbirds." "This is a song for all those convention-eers," Seger said, referring to members of the Society of Automotive Engineers gathered for their annual convention. "It's about making cars in the '50s." In her Free Press review, Dana Jackson wrote: "Scorching solos from guitarist Craig Frost and saxophone player Alto Reed had even the most cautious Seger fan standing and shouting."

JOHN STANO/DETROIT FREE PRESS

NO. 15: FEB. 24, 1987
SEGER NEVER FORGETS

BOB SEGER ENDS HIS EPIC AMERICAN STORM TOUR WITH AN EPIC SERIES OF SHOWS IN DOWNTOWN DETROIT

Bob Seger may have opened his 1986 summer shows at Pine Knob Music Theatre with his latest single, "American Storm," but coming home in the dead of winter to close his long tour, Detroit's hometown favorite knew what to do. Seger hit The Joe's stage by punctuating the beat with a fist thrust and a roaring rendition of "Rock 'n' Roll Never Forgets." And the party was on.

A 2004 inductee to the Rock & Roll Hall of Fame, Seger, 41 at the time, played seven concerts over 13 nights at the end February and beginning of March. "With a 21-song set planned for seven nights of home-coming," the Free Press' Dana Jackson wrote, "the only advice for Seger fans is bring your memories and your dancing shoes."

NO. 16: DEC. 12, 1979
UNHYPED HOOPS

WOLVERINES, TITANS AND ONLY 12,319 FANS CHRISTEN AN ARENA CRITICIZED AS UNFINISHED AND UNSAFE BY ARCHITECTS

Detroit's new riverfront arena opened with a college basketball game pitting the Michigan Wolverines against the University of Detroit Titans. The Wolverines (4-1) trounced the Titans (2-3), 85-72, behind 36 points (on 15-for-29 shooting) and 10 rebounds (a game high) from Mike McGee (pictured above).

Only 12,319 fans turned out for the first event at the 20,000-seat Joe Louis Arena, which still wasn't finished 15 days before the Red Wings, its main tenant, were to leave Olympia to start playing by the Detroit River. Seating sections were marked with chalk, many seats had yet to be numbered, and tempo-rary concession stands had to be set up. Price check: 50 cents for a Coke, 75 cents for carmel corn and $2.25 for a 24-ounce brew.

The fans, though, didn't complain too much about the massive 36-step outdoor stairways that led to the main entrances, the topic of reports in the Free Press and Detroit News that they weren't safe. Each newspaper retained an architect to critique the new arena. Lyndon Welch, a retired Harvard- and MIT-trained architect-civil engineer, told Free Press read-ers that the city should re-move about 500 top-row seats for easier access to emergen-cy exits and enclose the entrance stairs because of the inherent dangers of wintry weather. He also said he was "very uncomfortable" with holding the basketball game because the arena looked "at least" a month away from completion.

Fans close to the court, who paid $11, were mostly happy with their vantage points. Fans seated nearer to the top of the 42-row sides, who paid $10, complained about the distance. "Everybody looks like an ant if you don't have binoculars," said Shirley Lewis of Detroit. "This to me is as bad as the Silverdome."

At halftime, Mayor Coleman Young called Joe and Martha Louis in Las Vegas from the press room. "I thought you or Joe might be disturbed," Young told Martha, "because we've had some bad press" about the arena. Louis, who worked in the 1970s as a casino greeter until serious health issues, died of cardiac arrest at 66 on April 12, 1981, never having set foot in his namesake arena.

Ol' Blue Eyes

The massive snowstorm in the hours before Frank Sinatra's concert at The Joe was so bad that banks and malls dismissed employees early, federal and county offices closed early, and Detroit public schools, which just had reopened after closing for two days because of the last storm, sent students home early and canceled classes for the following day. But Diane Haithman wrote in the Free Press: "For the many who made it … Sinatra's way was just right. From inside of this polished performance, we couldn't even tell it was cold."
JOHN COLLIER/DETROIT FREE PRESS

NO. 17: FEB. 3, 1982
THE SHOW MUST GO ON — MOSTLY
SINATRA DID IT HIS WAY — AND THAT WAS RIGHT ON THE MARK FOR LUCKY FANS

Frank Sinatra canceled his concert during Super Bowl week — the 49ers would beat the Bengals — because of the flu. Two weeks later, the rescheduled date fell during a major winter storm, Detroit's second in four days. How bad was it? The State Police warned motorists to stay off the roads except for emergencies.

Still, Sinatra, then 66, decided the show must go on. He had arrived a day earlier to beat the snow, holed up in a downtown hotel, ate barbecued ribs and eventually told the 12,000 to 14,000 fans at The Joe: "I wouldn't have come out to see anyone tonight — even me!"

Another 6,000 to 8,000 fans who paid between $15 and $25 for tickets either never made it to the arena or decided to heed the police warnings. Arena officials declared no refunds would be forthcoming and another postponement was impractical, because the following night the Wings were scheduled at home and the Chairman of the Board had a benefit performance in Los Angeles.

The Free Press' Diane Haithman wrote: "Sinatra's formality soon dissolved into a sort of stiff whimsicality — although his trademark is a mellow, understated class, he clearly displayed a playful enjoyment of his songs and the hypnotic nostalgia they induced in his audience. He may have missed a lyric or two (the audience liked that better than anything) but he never missed a beat. … There was no

special treatment given the audience because of the snow. The performance was short — 50 minutes, no encore — even with a standing ovation and thunderous applause, when Frank wants to go home, he goes home."

Sinatra received much more favorable reviews for two later concerts at The Joe: in 1988 on the Together Again Tour with Sammy Davis Jr. (Dean Martin had dropped out by the Detroit engagement) and in 1991 during his Diamond Jubilee World Tour (with special guests Steve Lawrence and Eydie Gormé). In the latter, Sinatra toasted the crowd with the brew of his sponsor, Chivas Regal: "May you live to be 775 years old and the last voice you hear is mine!"

Madonna in Motown

Madonna long had used her tours to emphasize her latest music, in this case "Rebel Heart" material. Her classics got nipped and tucked inside other numbers. The Free Press' Brian McCollum gave the concert a thumbs-up: "Thursday brought a lean-and-lithe Madonna who balanced seriously intense performances with a lighthearted, sometimes mischievous spirit. For all the sizzle — the dazzling set pieces, the splashy visuals, the eye-popping interludes by her supremely skilled dance crew — it was a show that planted some genuine heart in the proceedings."

KIMBERLY P. MITCHELL/DETROIT FREE PRESS

NO. 18: OCT. 1, 2015
WHO'S THAT GIRL?
MATERIAL GIRL EMBRACES HER MOTOWN ROOTS

Madonna's first tour — 1985's The Virgin Tour — included back-to-back nights at Cobo Arena and a widely popular VHS concert video filmed in Detroit. Over the next two decades, she often was accused of spurning her Michigan roots — born in Bay City, grew up Madonna Louise Ciccone in Pontiac and Rochester Hills, and attended the University of Michigan. Oh, she played the Palace of Auburn Hills a couple of times — including a live concert for HBO during her 2001 Drown World Tour — and The Joe in 2012, but a truly Detroit-centric show didn't arrive until 2015 at the riverfront arena.

Five months earlier, Madonna told Us Weekly there was "nothing at all" she missed about growing up in Michigan and savaged her hometown on Howard Stern's radio show. "Have you have been to Rochester Hills, Mich.," she told the shock jock. "I can't be around basic, provincial-thinking peo-

ple." The last comment prompted the town's mayor, Bryan Barnett, to write an open letter to the pop superstar. "It's like someone calling one of your kids ugly," Barnett told the Free Press. "People were kind of surprised, because it did seem like she was re-embracing the area."

Madonna did that and more at The Joe. She included pep talks about Detroit's resilience, celebrations of the city's comeback ("Watch out!"), mentions of her charity involvement in an after-school touring program at the Downtown Boxing Gym and job training for homeless women in the Empowerment Plan, and even a shout-out to developer and "incredible guy" Dan Gilbert.

"Motor City, your hometown girl is back," declared Madonna, 57. In the sold-out crowd were her 84-year-old father, Silvio Ciccone, and her daughter, Lourdes Leon, a sophomore at U-M.

NO. 19: JUNE 12, 1981
THROWING IN THE TOWEL ON DEDICATING THE JOE
FRIDAY NIGHT FIGHTS: LITTLE ACTION, NO DEDICATION

For the first time in 11 years, the heavyweight boxing championship was on the line in the Motor City. This time, it was in the new arena named after a great heavyweight champion. The nationally televised fight, however, wasn't a thriller: Champion Larry Holmes scored a third-round TKO over past champion Leon Spinks.

In typical fight fashion — and Detroit fashion — the out-of-ring story lines were more dramatic than the action in the squared circle.

For starters, to boost attendance, promoters sold the event as a tribute to Joe Louis and promised an official ceremony to dedicate the 18-month-old arena. Fingers were

CONTINUED ON PAGE 121

When the referee mercifully stopped the bout, champion Larry Holmes had pinned Leon Spinks in the corner for the final onslaught. Spinks often must have felt like throwing in the towel after moving to Detroit as heavyweight champion in 1978. He had his front teeth stolen in a 1980 mugging. He lost his ring mementos because of a dispute with a moving company in 1985. His skills eroded, he accepted a job as a bartender in 1988.

ALAN R. KAMUDA/DETROIT FREE PRESS

A taste of leather

Champion Larry Holmes dominated Leon Spinks from the opening bell. George Puscas wrote in the Free Press: "Holmes' greater size, speed and strength, which were expected to be decisive, proved too much for Spinks. Poor Leon. He tried mightily, but he simply did not have the equipment or the talent to threaten Holmes, and his bid to regain the heavyweight title he had won from Muhammad Ali collapsed almost before it began."

TONY SPINA/DETROIT FREE PRESS

CONTINUED FROM PAGE 120

pointed in every direction why it didn't happen as planned at 7:30 p.m. before a lightweight undercard bout. A publicist with Don King Promotions said Mayor Coleman Young showed up late. Coleman said Martha Louis, Joe's widow who had been flown in from Las Vegas with their four adopted children, couldn't be located. Local promoter Edward Bell said Louis was "a little upset" but ABC-TV "made changes we didn't know about."

An announcement informed fans that the ceremony would be delayed until after the main event. But Young refused to allow it then because fans were leaving. "I didn't want to dedicate the arena looking at peoples' backs," he said.

As fans exited, ushers handed out souvenir programs that said: "Joe Louis Sports Arena, Detroit, Mich. Dedicated June 12, 1981, to the memory of Joe Louis (Barrow)." One usher said: "They can plastic-coat this and hang it on the wall. Then they can't say this place ain't dedicated no more."

Unbeaten in his 38 fights, Holmes bloodied the lip of Howard Cosell, the mouth of television. During an interview, Cosell pointed to contender Gerry Cooney — labeled "The Great White Hope" — and asked Holmes when he would fight him. "Get that guy out of here!" Holmes hollered, waving his arm wildly. The arm crashed into Cosell's microphone, and the microphone slammed into his mouth, cutting his lip.

Spinks, a Marine from St. Louis with missing front teeth, won a gold medal at the 1976 Montreal Olympics and the heavyweight title from Muhammad Ali in 1978 in his eighth pro fight. He then moved to a $75,000 split-level home in Detroit's Rosedale Park with his wife. By year's end, he had lost a rematch with Ali. In his adopted home, Spinks became best known for hanging out at the Last Chance Bar, a bizarre mugging in 1981 and missing choppers.

He told police he was robbed of a full-length blue fox coat, jewelry and a dental plate with four upper teeth —

a $45,000 loss. He told police that an unseen attacker struck him on his head about 11:30 p.m. while he was leaving Spears Bar on Woodward near 6 Mile. Spinks said he was naked in the Crestwood Motor Hotel five miles away when he regained consciousness 13 hours later. The Free Press could not find anyone who saw Spinks at Spears, but the Last Chance manager, Tom Tappelletti, said Spinks arrived at his Woodward and 8 Mile bar at 4 p.m. and didn't leave until closing time. "He was pretty well looped when he left," Tappelletti said. He thought it was with a woman and possibly two men. Police, though, said Spinks also was seen at the Booby Trap, another 8 Mile bar, shortly after 1 a.m.

The Free Press had this headline three days after the mugging: "Spinks' teeth found under bed in motel." A few weeks later, the Free Press reported that Spinks hadn't bothered to pick up his teeth, which had been stored in a brown envelope, and failed to show up to look at mug shots.

NO. 20: OCT. 8, 1983
UPGRADES AT THE JOE
ILITCH SHOWS OFF FIXES AT DEDICATION, AND STEVIE Y MAKES HIS HOME DEBUT

The Sunday that Joe Louis died in Las Vegas in 1981, the Brewster Old Timers were meeting in Detroit to arrange, at long last, "a program, a grand opening" for the 16-month-old riverfront area that bore his name.

"We got home to learn that Joe had died," said William O. Hines, president of the Old Timers, a collection of 190 former athletes who spent their childhood running, boxing and shooting baskets at Detroit's old Brewster Center, where the Brown Bomber learned to fight.

Louis, 66, collapsed walking to his bathroom at 9:45 a.m. on April 12. He was pronounced dead of cardiac arrest 20 minutes later at Desert Springs Hospital. An aneurysm, followed quickly by a stroke, essentially ended his public career in 1977 and left him virtually helpless and confined to his bedroom about a mile from The Strip, where he had worked as a Caesars Palace greeter.

However, the night before his death, Louis watched from a wheelchair at Caesars Palace's ringside as Larry Holmes successfully defended his title against Trevor Berbick. Ten days earlier, Louis had been feted by 1,500 people, including many former boxing greats.

The Brewster Old Timers hadn't given up hope that someday — maybe in the fall of '81 — Louis could return to Detroit for an arena dedication.

Even after Louis' death, talk of dedicating The Joe never went away. This idea and that idea were floated. A ceremony even was scheduled the night of Holmes' bout with Leon Spinks in June 1981. Louis' widow, Martha, and their children were flown to town. Hines was to introduce the mayor and help present that plaque that would hang outside the building. But at the last minute, the event was scrapped.

Who could make it happen? Mike Ilitch, the Red Wings' new owner.

The dedication was scheduled for opening night of the Wings' 1983-84 season. The arena had been in business nearly four years and Louis had been dead for 2½.

The team's largest opening-night crowd, 18,956, drank in the glitzy pregame bash, yelled loudly for boxing champion Thomas Hearns, booed Mayor Coleman Young and cheered a flying octopus.

The Wings lost, 6-3 to the New Jersey Devils. Steve Yzerman, an 18-year-old rookie center, made his home debut, assisting on their first goal, by Greg Smith, and their last goal, by Eddie Johnstone.

The Free Press' Bill McGraw described his first point at The Joe this way: "Finally, Greg Smith put a blue-line drive past (Ron) Lowe, the result of digging by Paul Woods and Steve Yzerman. That gave the Wings a short-lived lead, and brought a dead octopus flying out of the stands and flopping onto the ice, a re-creation of an old and bizarre local hockey rite usually associated with playoff wins."

Also that night, Ilitch unveiled a slew of off-season improvements to The Joe, including new lighting, fixtures, paint, murals, food stands and a marble-based memorial to the man who held the heavyweight crown for 12 years. "I want to warm that building up," Ilitch said. "I want to beautify it for the city, but mainly for the fans."

Joe Louis would have appreciated it.

NO. 21: JULY 6, 2000
A SMOKING COURT CASE
A HIP-HOP TOUR'S DETROIT STOP TURNS INTO AN 11-YEAR LEGAL SKIRMISH

The Up in Smoke hip-hop tour traveled the country for three weeks without a hitch — until it arrived in Michigan for back-to-back performances at The Joe and the Palace of Auburn Hills.

The events that unfolded at The Joe led to a series of legal maneuvers that lasted 11 years. At first, the issue was a seven-minute video to be shown during the concert with Dr. Dre and Snoop Dogg lounging with topless women and a shoot-'em-up liquor store robbery. Eventually, the Michigan Supreme Court ruled that Detroit city officials had no right to privacy when they were videotaped backstage at the 2000 concert.

The brouhaha started as a free-speech confrontation between Mayor Dennis Archer's office and the national tour, which Magic Johnson promoted. (He was even backstage for both Michigan concerts.) The tour featured rap superstars Eminem, Dr. Dre, Snoop Dogg, Ice Cube and Nate Dogg.

Greg Bowens, a spokesman for Archer, and other city officials threatened to cut power and arrest organizers if the video were shown. Tour officials gave in.

That confrontation later was included in a tour DVD.

The next day, U.S. District Judge Nancy Edmunds ruled that Auburn Hills officials had no right to interfere with showing the video at that night's concert at the Palace. The ruling notwithstanding, policed ticketed Dr. Dre for promotion of pornography.

Herschel Fink, a lawyer specializing in First Amendment issues, filed civil-rights

The real Slim Shady

Eminem played a role in the Up In Smoke Tour's dustup with Detroit officials. They balked at his plan to carry an unclothed inflatable doll onto the stage during his half-hour set. Already facing a court appearance the next day in Macomb County on gun charges, the rapper gave in.
NOLAN WELLS/DFP

suits for Dr. Dre against Detroit and Auburn Hills. A year later, the mayors apologized, the cities handed over roughly $25,000 apiece for attorney fees and the suits were dropped.

However, in 2002, five current or former Detroit officials, including Bowens, sued Dr. Dre — and virtually anyone else associated with the tour DVD, including Johnson — for invading their privacy, in part by using "a hidden camera and microphones." Fink, who also represented the Free Press in editorial matters, called the charges "basically comic." The plaintiffs' attorney, Glenn Oliver, said the damages in the case could reach $3 billion. Fink countered: "He will not get three cents."

A series of rulings over the years bounced the case around in circuit court, the appellate court and eventually the state Supreme Court. Fink argued that there was no privacy when police were doing their jobs and that the city officials knew they were being filmed "because they were saying, 'Shut off the camera.'" In 2011, the high court agreed in a 6-1 decision.

NO. 22: JAN. 22, 1982
THE DIVA OF MOTOWN
DIANA ROSS UPSTAGES THE CHAIRMAN AND ROD THE BOD DURING SUPER BOWL WEEK

For Super Bowl XVI at the Pontiac Silverdome, four monster concerts were booked 30 miles away at The Joe to add to the glamour and hype. The first, by Frank Sinatra on Wednesday night, was canceled because the Chairman had the flu. The last featured Rod Stewart on Sunday night, a few hours after the San Francisco 49ers and Joe Montana beat the Cincinnati Bengals, 26-21.

However, as she did so often, Diana Ross stole the headlines. Ross, at 37, performed two concerts Friday — scheduled for 8 p.m. and midnight. After growing up in Detroit's Brewster-Douglass housing projects, Ross came to fame in the 1960s with the Supremes for Berry Gordy's Motown Records and reached even greater heights as a solo artist — and iconic rock diva — in the 1970s.

"The glitter and razzmatazz in her performance was abundant," W. Kim Heron

wrote for the Free Press. "She came on stage in a jacket that seemed more like

Lady sings the blues

As the song said: No wind, no rain nor winter storm could keep fans from getting to Diana Ross during Super Bowl week. Though the weather outside was frightful, Detroit's super singer was delightful in front of a full house at The Joe. The Free Press wrote: "Ross gave the Super Bowl-saturated entertainment scene a much-needed dose of glamour."
HUGH GRANNUM/DETROIT FREE PRESS

a storm of feathers. There was a full-length sequined gown under that which gave way to pastel leotards later in the show. Near the finale, she pranced off stage and returned in a mass of something somewhere between lace frills and orange cotton candy. …

"The audience cheered wildly at the mere introduction of most tunes."

NO. 23: JUNE 13, 1987
OH, CANADA!
NHL'S FIRST DRAFT SOUTH OF THE BORDER STILL TURNS OUT TO BE CANADA'S PARTY

For the first time, the NHL's annual amateur draft was held outside Canada. While 5,000 fans munched on free Little Caesars pizza at The Joe, the league turned the clock back on two decades of expanding its talent pool from Canada to the United States and Europe.

In 1986, seven Americans — a record — were selected in the first round and six more Americans and three Finns went in the second round. In Detroit, all 21 players selected in the first round were born in Canada. Seventeen Canadians were selected in the second round and 18 more in the third round. Swedish defenseman Ricard Persson — No. 23 overall — was the first non-Canadian drafted. Right wing John LeClair — No. 33 overall — was the first American drafted.

The Buffalo Sabres used the No. 1 pick on center Pierre Turgeon from the Granby Bisons of the Quebec Major Junior Hockey League. In 2005, he would become the 34th player to score 500 goals. He spent 19 seasons in the NHL (with the Sabres, Islanders, Canadiens, Blues, Stars and Avalanche), finishing with 515

goals and 812 assists, four All-Star Game appearances and the 1993 Lady Byng Trophy. Two players from the draft class

No. 1 with a bullet

With the NHL draft at The Joe, Shawn Burr dropped by to congratulate the Red Wings' latest first-round choice, Yves Racine. A defenseman from Matane, Quebec, Racine was the 11th player selected. "It was a surprise for me to be selected in the first round of the draft," he said. Burr, a forward from Sarnia, Ontario, who was the No. 7 pick in 1984, was coming off a season in which he finished fifth for the Selke Trophy as top defensive forward.
MARY SCHROEDER/DFP

have reached the Hockey Hall of Fame: former Red Wing Brendan Shanahan, drafted second overall by the New Jersey Devils, and Joe Sakic, drafted 15th overall by the Quebec Nordiques.

The Wings could have skipped the draft. They used the 11th pick on French-Canadian defenseman Yves Racine, who spent parts of four undistinguished seasons with the team. Their other 12 draft picks played a total of 31 games for the Winged Wheel.

A DIAMOND IS A JOE'S BEST FRIEND

IN THE ARENA'S EARLY DAYS, NOBODY PACKED 'EM IN AS OFTEN AS THE SINGER-SONGWRITER ONCE NICKNAMED 'THE JEWISH ELVIS'

Sweet Caroline, ba, ba, ba ...

How popular was Neil Diamond in the 1980s? Even though he always was one of those artists that you either loved or hated, Diamond sold almost 100,000 tickets for a 1983 long weekend at The Joe — concerts Thursday, Friday, Saturday and Sunday nights, plus a Sunday matinee. In 1982, Diamond had done three shows in three nights at The Joe. In 1985, he would perform four in four nights.

During L.A. rehearsals for the '83 tour, Diamond told the Free Press that he could not explain his popularity across all demographics. "As soon as I figure it out," he said, "I'll do more of whatever brings them out. I'm just thankful, really."

Songs sung blue

During his long weekends at The Joe, Neil Diamond didn't cut corners. He always was a hardworking showman who belted out his hits with an enthusiasm unknown to mankind. At The Joe in 1983, he started with "America" and finished 33 songs later with "America (Reprise)." Along the way, he launched into perennial favorites such as "Solitary Man," "Kentucky Woman," "Sweet Caroline" and "Brother Love's Traveling Salvation Show."

DETROIT FREE PRESS

Black empowerment

For 2½ hours, Minister Louis Farrakhan, leader of the Nation of Islam, addressed the multitudes at The Joe. Farrakhan said he had met the previous day with Detroit Police Chief James Craig to discuss reducing violence and the issue of police abuse. The father of Michael Brown, killed by police in Ferguson, Mo., in 2014, was at the rally, on stage behind Farrakhan. "He's a good man," the minister said of the police chief. "I really like him." Farrakhan said he told Craig: "All of the rogue cops are found in the ghettos, so we're going to help you. We're going to find them and point them out. We're not going to kill them, but we're going to give you a chance to take them off the streets, bust them and try them and sentence them."

TIM GALLOWAY/DETROIT FREE PRESS

NO. 25: FEB. 21, 2016
DETROIT HOSTS A NATION
NATION OF ISLAM CELEBRATES IN THE CITY WHERE THE ORGANIZATION STARTED IN 1930

Minister Louis Farrakhan, the 82-year-old leader of the Nation of Islam, called upon African Americans to unite and to help rebuild Detroit. During the last day of the group's annual convention, Farrakhan spoke for 2½ hours to more than 14,000 people at The Joe. He compared American sports to slavery, defended Beyonce's controversial performance at the 2016 Super Bowl, criticized Arab-American store owners who work in black neighborhoods, blasted the Republican and Democratic parties, referred to areas like Detroit and Harlem as oppressed "colonies," and called for the U.S. to be strongly defended against Islamic radical terrorists.

In the summer of 1930, an Asian man named Wallace Fard Muhammad arrived in Detroit and started preaching in African-American neighborhoods such as Black Bottom. His speeches asserted that black people were part of a superior race. The Nation of Islam, a group founded in Detroit that grew into the biggest black nationalist organization in the U.S. still existing today, developed from his teachings.

Now based in Chicago and led by Farrakhan, the Nation of Islam usually held its conventions in the Windy City. But it came to Detroit in 2014 and again in 2016. Farrakhan had been encouraging Nation of Islam members and others to move to the Motor City. His message of black self-empowerment resonated during frequent visits to the city, attracting crowds that went well beyond his Muslim base.

During his Saviours' Day keynote address, Farrakhan said: "Pool our resources. The opportunity is here, but the disunity is also here. Detroit can be the new Mecca. Detroit can be a great, great city again. You don't have to move out to the white community. Instead of moving out of the 'hood, let's make the 'hood what we desire it to be."

BY THE NUMBERS

THE SEASONS

Entering the 2016-17 season, the Wings had won 818 of their 1,425 games at The Joe, losing 417 times and getting a point from a tie or an overtime loss in 190 others. The breakdown:

SEASON	GP	W	L	T	OT	PTS
1979-80	28	8	17	3	—	19
1980-81	40	16	15	9	—	41
1981-82	40	15	19	6	—	36
1982-83	40	14	19	7	—	35
1983-84	40	18	20	2	—	38
1984-85	40	19	14	7	—	45
1985-86	40	10	26	4	—	24
1986-87	40	20	14	6	—	46
1987-88	40	24	10	6	—	54
1988-89	40	20	14	6	—	46
1989-90	40	20	14	6	—	46
1990-91	40	26	14	0	—	52
1991-92	40	24	12	4	—	52
1992-93	42	25	14	3	—	53
1993-94	42	23	13	6	—	52
1994-95	24	17	4	3	—	37
1995-96	41	36	3	2	—	74
1996-97	41	20	12	9	—	49
1997-98	41	25	8	8	—	58
1998-99	41	27	12	2	—	56
1999-00	41	28	9	3	1	60
2000-01	41	27	9	3	2	59
2001-02	41	28	7	5	1	62
2002-03	41	28	6	5	2	63
2003-04	41	30	7	4	0	64
2005-06	41	27	9	—	5	59
2006-07	41	29	4	—	8	66
2007-08	41	29	9	—	3	61
2008-09	41	27	9	—	5	59
2009-10	41	25	10	—	6	56
2010-11	41	21	14	—	6	48
2011-12	41	31	7	—	3	65
2012-13	24	13	7	—	4	30
2013-14	41	18	13	—	10	46
2014-15	41	22	10	—	9	53
2015-16	41	22	13	—	6	50

21-heart salute

On Valentine's Day in 2012, the Wings dimmed the Dallas Stars, 3-1, for their 21st straight victory at The Joe. Started on Nov. 5, 2011, the streak reached 23 on Feb. 19, 2012, but ended four days later with a shootout loss to Vancouver.
KIRTHMON F. DOZIER/DETROIT FREE PRESS

THE STREAK

The Wings set a franchise record during the 2011-12 season for consecutive home wins, going more than four months without a loss at home. The 23 games:

NOV. 5: Ducks, 5-0
NOV. 8: Avalanche, 5-2
NOV. 11: Oilers, 3-0
NOV. 12: Stars, 5-2
NOV. 23: Flames, 5-3
NOV. 26: Predators, 4-1
NOV. 30: Lightning, 4-2
DEC. 8: Coyotes, 5-2
DEC. 10: Jets, 7-1
DEC. 17: Kings, 8-2
DEC. 27: Blues, 3-2
DEC. 31: Blues, 3-0
JAN. 12: Coyotes, 3-2 (SO)
JAN. 14: Blackhawks, 3-2 (OT)
JAN. 16: Sabres, 5-0
JAN. 21: Blue Jackets, 3-2 (SO)
JAN. 23: Blues, 3-1
FEB. 8: Oilers, 4-2
FEB. 10: Ducks, 2-1 (SO)
FEB. 12: Flyers, 4-3
FEB. 14: Stars, 3-1
FEB. 17: Predators, 2-1
FEB. 19: Sharks, 3-2

HOLI-DAZED

Entering 2016-17, the Wings had a winning record at The Joe on 4 of 6 big dates:
LOSSES ARE COMBINED REGULATION AND OVERTIME LOSSES

HOME OPENERS	HALLOWEEN	NEW YEAR'S EVE
21-12-2	1-1-0	18-10-3

VALENTINE'S DAY	ST. PATRICK'S DAY	EASTER
5-4-1	5-3-0	0-3-1

TOURNEY TIME

A LOOK AT THE COLLEGE BASKETBALL AND HOCKEY TOURNAMENTS JOE LOUIS ARENA HOSTED OVER THE YEARS:

FROZEN FOUR

The Joe hosted college hockey's final four three times in a six-year span. The title games:

MARCH 30, 1985
RPI 2, PROVIDENCE 1: Future Red Wing Adam Oates won the title at Joe Louis Arena, but Friars goalie Chris Terreri became the first losing player named Most Outstanding Player since 1960.
THIRD PLACE: Minnesota-Duluth; **FOURTH PLACE:** Boston College.

MARCH 28, 1987
NORTH DAKOTA 5, MICHIGAN STATE 3:
Ron Mason and the Spartans just missed repeating as national champs at The Joe, losing to a Fighting Sioux team led by goalie Ed Belfour.
THIRD PLACE: Minnesota; **FOURTH PLACE:** Harvard.

APRIL 1, 1990
WISCONSIN 7, COLGATE 3: Wisconsin dominated the first Frozen Four to feature both semifinals played on the same day; five of the six members of the all-tournament team were Badgers.
THIRD PLACE: Boston College, Boston University

HORIZON LEAGUE HOOPS

The Horizon League, featuing Oakland and Detroit Mercy, moved its tournament to decide its NCAA tournament berth to Detroit in 2016. The results:
MARCH 5: No. 4 Green Bay beat No. 9 Cleveland State, 65-53
MARCH 5: No. 5 Milwaukee beat No. 8 Northern Kentucky, 86-69
MARCH 5: No. 3 Wright State beat No. 10 UIC, 74-43
MARCH 5: No. 6 Detroit Mercy beat No. 7 Youngstown St., 92-79
MARCH 6: No. 4 Green Bay beat No. 5 Milwaukee, 70-61
MARCH 6: No. 3 Wright State beat No. 6 Detroit Mercy, 82-72
MARCH 7: No. 4 Green Bay beat No. 1 Valparaiso, 99-92 (OT)
MARCH 7: No. 3 Wright State beat No. 2 Oakland, 59-55
MARCH 8: No. 4 Green Bay beat No. 3 Wright State, 78-69

BIG TEN HOCKEY

The Joe hosted the Big Ten's tournament to decide its NCAA berth in 2015 and 2017. The 2015 results:
MARCH 19: No. 5 Ohio State beat No. 4 Penn State, 3-1
MARCH 19: No. 3 Michigan beat No. 6 Wisconsin, 5-1
MARCH 20: No. 1 Minnesota beat No. 5 Ohio State, 3-0
MARCH 20: No. 3 Michigan beat No. 2 Michigan State, 4-1
MARCH 21: No. 1 Minnesota beat No. 3 Michigan, 4-2

GLI

The Joe hosted the Great Lakes Invitational, an annual college hockey tournament featuring Michigan, Michigan State, Michigan Tech and a fourth school, for all but one year since 1979. (The tourney was played outdoors at Comerica Park in 2013, with Western Michigan winning under the lights.) Michigan was the top winner, with 15 titles. Michigan State won it 11 times. The winners at The Joe:
2016: Western Michigan
2015: Michigan
2014: Michigan
2012: Michigan Tech
2011: Michigan
2010: Michigan
2009: Michigan State
2008: Michigan
2007: Michigan
2006: Michigan State
2005: Colorado College
2004: Michigan State
2003: Boston College
2002: Boston University
2001: North Dakota
2000: Michigan State
1999: Michigan State
1998: Michigan State
1997: Michigan State
1996: Michigan
1995: Michigan
1994: Michigan
1993: Michigan
1992: Michigan
1991: Michigan
1990: Michigan
1989: Michigan
1988: Michigan
1987: Wisconsin
1986: Western Michigan
1985: Michigan State
1984: Michigan State
1983: Michigan State
1982: Michigan State
1981: Notre Dame
1980: Michigan Tech
1979: Michigan Tech

CCHA

When Michigan, Michigan State, Michigan Tech and Notre Dame joined the Central Collegiate Hockey Association for the 1981-82 season, the annual tournament to decide the conference's NCAA tournament berth was moved to The Joe. (The tournament left after U-M and MSU left the conference in 2013.) The winners:
2013: Notre Dame
2012: Western Michigan
2011: Miami (Ohio)

2010: Michigan
2009: Notre Dame
2008: Michigan
2007: Notre Dame
2006: Michigan State
2005: Michigan
2004: Ohio State
2003: Michigan
2002: Michigan
2001: Michigan State
2000: Michigan State
1999: Michigan
1998: Michigan State
1997: Michigan
1996: Michigan
1995: Lake Superior State
1994: Michigan
1993: Lake Superior State
1992: Lake Superior State
1991: Lake Superior State
1990: Michigan State
1989: Michigan State
1988: Bowling Green
1987: Michigan State
1986: Western Michigan
1985: Michigan State
1984: Michigan State
1983: Michigan State
1982: Michigan State

RIP, Joe Louis Arena

The Red Wings played their first game at Joe Louis Arena along the Detroit River on Dec. 27, 1979. Their last regular-season game at The Joe was scheduled for April 9, 2017. The Wings planned to move a few miles to the new Little Caesars Arena for the 2017-18 season.

KIRTHMON F. DOZIER/DETROIT FREE PRESS